How to Grow Your Preschool into a Multi-Million Dollar Childcare Business Empire

I0466542

"How to Grow Your Preschool into a Multi-Million Dollar Childcare Business Empire"

Copyright Notice

Limits of Liability / Disclaimer of Warranty

Preschool Growth Plan: Table of Contents

I. Introduction

The objective of this book is to guide daycare and preschool operators on how-to improve the viability and profitability of their child care businesses for the following reasons:

1. According to the latest research, the global Early Childhood Education market size was valued at USD 465642.61 million in 2022 and is expected to expand at a CAGR of 7.51% during the forecast period, reaching USD 718843.49 million by 2028.
    Resource:
    www.thebrainyinsights.com/report/early-childhood-education-market-12703
2. The increasing workforce participation among parents, especially the mother.
3. The lack of reliable and quality infant and toddler child care is costing working parents, employers and taxpayers $122 billion annually in lost earnings, productivity and revenue, according to a 2024 report from business leader membership group ReadyNation.
4. There is a growing body of data that supports the benefits of structured early learning experiences for children.
5. The development of new revenue streams, and implementation of efficient operating and marketing strategies, will help childcare businesses to become more affordable and accessible to both lower- and middle-income families.
6. The education sector remains resistant to the fluctuations caused by normal business cycles or recessions.
7. Parents are able to realize savings by getting their children on the right learning path, at a young age, and lessening the need for more expensive educational interventions later in the child's life.

What is Important to Preschool Parents?

Research indicates that preschool parents are interested in the following requirements and preferred services, as a total packaged offering:
1. Licensing compliance with the basic standards of operating a preschool program, including health and safety rules, teacher-child ratios, group size, emergency plans, and staffing credentialling requirements.
2. Access to shared videos and photos
3. Access to digital documentation
4. Parent communication apps
5. Availability of standardized preschool quality assessments for comparison purposes.
6. Contactless check-in process
7. Use of online invoicing and automatic payment systems
8. Expanded range of educational activities and content for classrooms.
9. Continuous professional development of the early childhood educators
10. Authentic in-house assessment tool that teachers can objectively use to track the children's progress.
11. A clear set of documented administrative policies that outlines things like nutrition, hygiene, procedures for incidents, progress reports, etc.

12.	A learning environment, that is, safe and has developmentally appropriate materials, to provide children with opportunities to interact with their environment in age- and developmentally-appropriate ways.
13.	Guidance on how-to satisfy children's emotional, behavioral, educational and physical unmet needs.
	Resource:
	www.moms.com/unmet-needs-school-aged-kids-have-parents-overlook/

# II.	Rethink the Program Blending Possibilities

Offer Uniquely Blended Education Philosophies
We will develop a blended approach that utilizes the best practices of several education philosophy-based programs, to create a distinctive competitive advantage. We will also describe the key learning method differences with parents so they can appreciate our superior approach to child development, and let them make an informed choice as to the blended method they prefer for their child.

Traditional Preschool
In a traditional preschool, the teacher is the central figure in the classroom and guides the children through various station or group activities. The teacher ensures that all the children meet the guidelines set by the school or determined by the curriculum. Children will rotate through activity centers, designated for different types of play or skills, as well as participate in group activities, like story time or art. Traditional preschool classrooms are usually filled with more colorful toys, and brightly colored posters, wall decorations, rugs, tables, and chairs. The shelves are filled with toys, games, and other familiar items. There is more of a focus on group activities, for structured social development purposes. The traditional preschool follows a linear progression, covering predetermined topics, regardless of children's cultural backgrounds, interests or experiences.

Montessori Program	**https://montessori-ami.org/visit-us**
	https://amshq.org/About-AMS/Contact
In a Montessori classroom the teacher acts as a guide, and follows the lead of the children. They learn at their own pace and are also guided by their individualized interests and sense of curiosity. This means that children are free to make choices about how they spend their time, but it must be done within the boundaries set by the teacher. In a Montessori school, "practical life work" that relates to the real world is stressed. Teachers invite children to a lesson, and show them how to use the materials independently. Learning is accomplished by doing or actually working with the materials. Activities are focused on sensory development at an early age. In a Montessori classroom, children are engaged in math, language, art, and geography studies, that they have chosen to work at themselves, and, consequently, become more invested in it. Montessori classrooms are usually decorated with more muted tones and have less visual stimulation. Classrooms use shapeable learning materials to help the children explore new passions, concepts, and skills, in a hands-on learning approach. The classroom is

often free of desks, with uninterrupted sessions for the students. This learning method incorporates global leadership, social justice, and promoting constructive conflict resolution. It emphasizes self-motivation through individualized learning. Montessori schools nurture children from infancy and early childhood, until the adolescent stage.

Examples: https://www.swmontessori.com/
                    https://www.cadence-education.com/programs/montessori/
Source: https://www.ourkids.net/school/criticisms-montessori-answered

STEM

This program encourages children to use a scientific perspective in their play and learning endeavors. It helps children to develop positive attitudes about the science and math fields, because it allows them to engage in those content areas in new ways. When participating in STEM experiences, children develop new habits and behaviors, such as asking questions, making observations, identifying problems, and sharing solutions.

Resources: https://www.seedsofstem.org/about
www.teacherspayteachers.com/browse?search=stem%20curriculum%20for%20preschool

High Scope
https://highscope.org/product-category/curriculum/preschool-curriculum-curriculum/
This program uses active learning and evidence-backed practices to engage children and establish school readiness skills. It provides an all-around learning environment, where children are encouraged to explore learning materials and interact with peers and adults. In a High Scope classroom, children are guided to explore, interact, and exercise their creative imagination through purposeful and pretend play, so they can have fun as they learn. In this program, children are exposed to an environment that fosters the development of cognitive skills and builds cultural, emotional, and social bonds. The classroom becomes a community where everyone watches out for each other. This early childhood education program relies on key development indicators to guide teachers in choosing the appropriate projects and activities for different ages. This makes it easy for teachers to understand and interpret the needs of children and customize their teaching to these particular needs. The center of this model is play. A teacher will act as the child's partner in a "play, do, review" sequence. The play-do review is unique to High Scope, where children choose activity plan goals to reach and work with teachers to evaluate the results.

Example:
The Kreative Kids Learning Center   https://kreativekidzlc.wixsite.com/kreative-kidz

Reggio Emilia   **https://www.reggiochildren.it/en/reggio-emilia-approach/**
This is a project-based learning approach, whereby preschoolers learn by exploring ideas and working on project-based activities, through the atelier (creative space) and the atelierista (artistic teacher). The system was developed to holistically enrich children, while factoring in their emotional and intellectual potential. It is a type of preschool program that incorporates an 'emergent curriculum' and encourages a child-centered approach. The objective is to create meaningful and engaging learning experiences that are open-ended, and revolve around a child's needs, skills, qualities, and interests. Educators observe children closely to understand their needs and strengths, and follow their lead when building classroom learning methodologies, and designing activities.

Classroom activities are often collaborative, allowing learners to form healthy relationships with the students. Children are encouraged to engage in active listening, participate in hands-on activities, and explore movement. Another feature of this approach is that the environment is considered to be a key educator in this learning style. The classroom learning is then supplemented by the direct involvement of the child's family and community, which are deemed to be critical to the child's learning journey and education success. The program offers monthly curriculum themes and social collaboration in various sized groups.
Examples:
Little Sunshine's Playhouse and Preschool   https://littlesunshine.com/
Cadence Education   www.cadence-education.com/programs/reggio-emilia/

Waldorf   https://www.waldorfeducation.org/waldorf-education
This preschool program, also known as Steiner Education, is a blend of structure and creative learning, with a focus on intellectual experimentation. Its educational style is holistic. It is intended to develop pupils' intellectual, artistic, and practical skills, with the focus being on imagination and creativity. Classrooms are often mixed-age and feature a play-based approach to learning. Its objective is to build learners' practical and art skills. Its philosophy strives to create a well-rounded individual. The Waldorf approach emphasizes the outdoors and creativity, instead of traditional academics. There are no assessments, tests, homework, or grading. Children undergo continuous testing through various activities. There is no set teaching method with this approach. Each learning institution that adopts the Waldorf approach, offers a unique teaching method and style. The typical school day involves personal contributions and collaborative learning, in small classroom settings, where the teacher watches over every child. Through creative learning, the child's daily activities are self-driven, and their lessons are mainly experiential. Waldorf is one of the early childhood education programs that drive a child's emotional, physical, and intellectual growth. Waldorf schools are available to children from kindergarten to the 12th grade.

Bank Street   https://www.bankstreet.edu/about-bank-street/our-approach/
https://school.bankstreet.edu/about/our-approach/
This approach is a non-traditional program that focuses on the social sciences. This model is active and imagination-based, and lets children learn from the environment around them. It focuses on the development of the whole child. It uses an interdisciplinary approach to subjects to allow children to engage in education emotionally. Bank Street preschool programs use a developmental-interaction approach that aims to develop the child physically, emotionally, socially, and intellectually. Children use different materials to learn in environments that accommodate their different stages of life. Classrooms are mixed-age with environments that match every learner's needs. Children socialize and work with different peers with the guidance of their facilitators. There is no competition among the learners. Students decide whether they want to learn using a hands-on approach or through observation. Teachers provide one-on-one attention with the learner's passion in mind.

Parent Cooperative Preschools   https://www.preschools.coop/

In this preschool program, parents and families are directly and actively involved in their child's education and learning. Cooperative preschools occur when like-minded parents join together to hire teachers who fit their children's learning styles. While the system emphasizes the value of education, it also grows the bond between parent and child. The teachers and parents work in tandem to ensure smooth learning processes. Parents are often present during teaching sessions, and will supervise their children. Typically, parents offer advice or contribute to the curriculum, sometimes assuming administrative roles, including assisting teachers with lessons. PCPI resolutely advocates that member preschools embrace play-based learning as the foundation of their educational philosophy. Hands-on experiences in creative arts, music, science, literature, and language are offered at developmentally appropriate levels.

Source:
Parent Cooperative Preschools International   https://www.preschools.coop/
PCPI is a non-profit international council, representing more than 50,000 families and teachers, which provides "on-going support to preschools, families, educators, and social agencies who recognize the value of parents as teachers of their children and the necessity of educating parents to meet the developmental needs of their children.
Resource: https://www.pgpedia.com/p/parent-cooperative-preschools-international

Ascend   **www.cadence-education.com/faqs/what-makes-the-ascend-curriculum-different-from-that-of-other-schools/**
This program is a combination of skills and play-based curriculum, that nurtures the student's social-emotional, physical, creative, and cognitive abilities. Children perform teacher-guided activities that encourage personalized interactions. Through personalization, children engage with others, while having fun and uncovering their passion for learning. They are encouraged to use critical thinking to find solutions to complex problems. This preschool curriculum offers a balance of structure and flexibility. Teachers offer a personalized approach to learning, and children are encouraged to create their own projects. The goal is to help students to build a strong foundation, as they develop vital skills, through the exercise of creativity.

Faith-based or Religious Preschools
Religious-based preschools incorporate theological themes into the children's learning sessions. Every religious preschool develops its philosophy according to its particular religion and its teachings. It aims to provide an environment where both teachers and children discuss their beliefs, openly while practicing their faith. Usually, a faith-based approach does not focus entirely on religion, but rather incorporates religious values into academic lessons. The religious preschool curriculum incorporates religious themes into the stories, songs, games, and other activities that the children play with.
Directory: https://www.care.com/christian-day-care
                  https://fun4seminolekids.com/Education-Childcare/Preschools-and-Child-Care-Centers-Faith-Based/
Resources:
https://mbskids.com/blog/what-are-the-different-preschool-curriculum-models/

Blended Preschool Curriculum Program

Our program will utilize the best practices of several curriculum styles, in the development of our own unique education philosophy. The proposed distinctive curriculum will be designed to encourage curiosity, exploration, language, physical and social development, and problem solving in a nurturing atmosphere, that shows respect for the learning abilities of each child. Teachers will personalize the curriculum and plan experiences based on children's interests and experiences, and teach appropriate educational concepts. Our goal is to be at the forefront of implementing technology integration into the early child learning process.

Example: https://kidsrkids.com/curriculum/

The key qualities of the blended program will be:
1.   Accommodates various interactive learning styles
2.   Meets the different needs of children
3.   Offers personalized activities
4.   Facilitates learning-by-doing, or experiential learning, via hands-on activities
5.   Encourages family engagement
6.   Shares the family's values
7.   Offers a creativity-inspiring learning environment
8.   Prepares the child for future academic and personal success
9.   Utilizes more digital tools and systems, and technological resources
10.   Focuses on learning through group teamwork in a cooperative manner
11.   Inspires co-participation of students within the teaching-learning process

Incorporate Other Learning Approaches

We will incorporate other learning approaches and models to create a uniquely differentiated and engaging learning experience for our students.

Universal Design for Learning Principles:
1.   Enable students to pursue deeper dive options, based on their interests.
2.   Provide a continuous source of feedback, to both families and students.
3.   Help students to set their own learning goals.
4.   Learn by doing refers to learning from hands-on experiences, and interacting with the environment to adapt and learn.

Game-Based Learning

This fun, play-based learning model involves using actual, competitive games, in a lesson plan, to improve learning engagement and motivation. This will involve both the playing of digital video games and traditional games. These games will support different student learning styles. To be effective, such educational media must remain open-ended, socially interactive, and flexible, while remaining responsive to the child's questions. Game playing will also support the development of fine motor skills, strengthen coordination, improve reaction time, and stimulate social and emotional development. The use of a computer touch screen will help to develop digital literacy, and require that the child's eyes and hands are working together to support fine motor development.

Source: www.edutopia.org/article/digital-resources-play-based-learning-preschool/
           https://mybrightwheel.com/blog/game-based-learning

Examples:

Happy Clicks www.happyclicks.net/click-tap-games/toddlers_games_objects2.php
Their website features age-appropriate entertaining free learning activities for young
children.

Stack the States   www.amazon.com/Dan-Russell-Pinson-Stack-the-States/
                       dp/B00DZYXTRY
It asks questions about state capital, landmarks, and identification of state flags. For each
question correctly answered, the user makes a stack of states until they are high enough to
pass a dotted line on the screen.

Turtle Diary   www.turtlediary.com/games/preschool.html
Their games help students build a foundation and achieve beyond all while having fun.

Collaborative Learning

A collaborative learning approach involves students working together on activities or
learning tasks in a small group, to accomplish a shared goal. The objective will be to
ensure that everyone participates. Students in the group may work on separate tasks,
contributing to a common overall outcome, or work together on a shared task, both of
which will foster teamwork, leadership skills, feelings of independence, and social
development. Cooperative play will result when children start working together towards a
common goal, such as building a block tower. Students who participate in group art
projects and school stage performances, usually benefit from these collaborative types of
learning experiences. To encourage cooperative learning, classroom seating will usually
be arranged in a circular layout, to enable more group discussions.
Resources:
www.wondertree.co/benefits-of-collaborative-learning-in-early-childhood-education/
https://montessori-academy.com/blog/cooperative-play-in-children/

Project-based Learning

This learning method involves students questioning, designing, developing, and
constructing hands-on solutions to a problem, in the real world. It aims to build students'
creative capacity to work collaboratively, through difficult problems, usually in small
teams, with supplied tools. Other developmental benefits include: critical thinking,
meaningful collaboration, logical reasoning, better engagement, perseverance,
communication skills and the fun factor. As an example, a gardening project can involve
counting seeds, preparing the soil, reading planting instructions, and watering and caring
for the plant, over an extended period of time. This can also reinforce math and literacy
skills, in a fun group engaging way.
Resource: https://mybrightwheel.com/blog/project-based-learning-preschool

Flex Teaching Model

We will facilitate different learning opportunities for students with different learning

capabilities and interests. We will use the following range of teaching methods, on an as-needed basis, to personalize the learning process and improve student engagement:
1. On-on-one tutoring
2. Small group instruction sessions
3. Project-based learning
4. Standard lectures

Rotation Teaching Model
According to this teaching model, students rotate on a fixed schedule or at the teacher's request, between learning modalities, which, at least one, involves online learning. It involves the traditional face-to-face learning with online learning. This method will provide teachers with constant information on the performance of their students, and allows for quick and easy modifications, if a student requires assistance.
Resource: https://www.plsclasses.com/blog/best-practices-for-educators/
                 understanding-the-rotational-model-of-learning/

Flipped Classroom Method
With this model, students will first watch pre-recorded, instructional videos at home, or other non-classroom settings, and then use customized, classroom-scheduled, time to work collaboratively on problem solving, with other students and teachers, in small group settings. Students will gain the necessary knowledge before class, and teachers will guide students to actively and interactively clarify and apply the home-acquired knowledge during class.
Source: https://www.panopto.com/blog/what-is-a-flipped-classroom/

Self-Blend Model
According to this model, individual students will decide the mix of online courses and on-campus, face-to-face teacher instruction. It gives students some autonomy to supplement in-school learning. In a true blended learning environment, both the student and the teacher should be physically located in the same space.
Source: https://learningdiscourses.com/discourse/self-blended-model-of-learning/

Blend Online Learning Programs
We will design traditional hands-on classroom experiences that are synchronized and optimized with online learning programs. Parents will also be able to monitor and track student's activities and work online. Our students will take online courses to learn the basics of a topic, and then attend in-person or face-to-face classes, to directly engage with certified teachers, to get their questions answered, and improve upon their skill sets.
The online tutoring for preschoolers will serve to introduce structure and undistracted focus to their daily routine. Virtual programs will combine live sessions with independent hands-on learning activities, which will provide a sense of stability and security that aids in developing independence and creativity in children.
Source: https://www.learnupon.com/blog/what-is-blended-learning/
                 https://empowerment.chrysalis.world/blog/how-to-create-a-lesson-plan-
                 format-for-a-blended-learning-setup
Resource: https://childrenshouse-montessori.com/2019/09/03/difference-between-

Offer a Blended Age Learning Environment

We will develop an apprenticeship program to teach the advanced older students to act as coaches to the younger children for the following reasons:

1. To build the self-confidence of the designated older coaching students.
2. To teach older students how to handle greater responsibilities.
3. To give older students a reason for receiving a higher level of recommendations.
4. To recognize the academic achievements of qualified older students.
5. To give younger students access to coaches that they identify with.
6. To teach younger students from a different perspective.

Offer Classes with Different Educational Philosophies

We will offer two programs, with different educational philosophies, such as Montessori and Reggio Emilia, and give parents the information to make an informed class selection decision.

Example: www.cadence-education.com/programs/

III. Focus on Developing Creative Intelligence

Empower Children to Develop Their Creative Intelligence

We will develop a learning environment that nurtures children's creative intelligence, by allowing them to think-outside-the-box, to solve problems. We will foster the development of creative thinking, which is the act of diverging one's thinking, to explore many different problem-solving options.

We will help children to develop their creative intelligence, for the following reasons:

1. To look at challenges with an open mind
2. To explore multiple solutions
3. To better adapt to changing circumstances.
4. To encourage self-expression.
5. To boost the self-confidence to explore new interests.
6. To promote a sense of curiosity.
7. To be able to embrace failure as a learning opportunity.
8. To thrive in the new world of AI, which demands creativity, innovation, and adaptability.

We will develop programs that help to build children's creative intelligence quotient in the following ways:

1. Conduct nature walks that encourage the asking of creation questions.
2. Stage sports activities that require creative body building movements.
3. Welcome the asking of open-ended questions.

4. Focus on the visual arts, including drawing, painting and sculpting pictures or designs from their imagination.
5. Practice seeing things from multiple perspectives by challenging assumptions.
6. Hold fun dance and singing activities, based on feeling and interpreting the music.
7. Provide a wide diversity of learning-by-doing experiences.
8. Encourage out-of-the-box approaches to creative problem solving and fixing things.
9. Ask children to see beyond conventional constraints, and to think of as many unusual uses for an object, as is possible.
10. Engage in more creative activities, such as art, music, storytelling, and problem-solving.
11. Produce and show tutorial videos that demonstrate the art of creatively making things, in a collaborative group setting.
12. Teach children that failure provides an acceptable approach to learning.
13. Ask children to use blocks to build a house that they would like to live in, and explain why the mentioned features are important to them.
14. Ask the children to draw pictures of ideas or things, that they are passionate about, and feature those drawings in design art exhibitions.
15. Introduce the children to a wide range of creativity-enabling materials, such as cardboard or PVC tubes, wood blocks, clay, paints, and fabric samples, and show examples of how past students have challenged norms.

Build a Makerspace Room

Makerspaces are public spaces located in schools, public libraries, and other community locations where people can meet up, share creative interests, explore new technologies, and learn by doing. Our Makerspace room will be a collaborative workspace that provides hands-on, creative ways to encourage students to problem solve, design, experiment, build and invent, as they engage in hands on learning, science, engineering and tinkering. We will build a Makerspace Room that facilities the development of creative thinking skills, and the use of collaboration in a group setting, to share talents and help each other to complete a STEM project that helps to develop critical thinking skills and boosts self-confidence. We will adapt a room to not only serve as the Makerspace Room, but also, as the library and party rental room.

Resources:	https://1stmakerspace.com/blog/starting-a-makerspace
https://www.facebook.com/groups/makerspaceorganizers/
Suppliers:	https://arcbotics.com/	www.makeblock.com
www.lego.com/en-us/aboutus	www.basicfun.com/
https://goldieblox.com/

Growth Trend:
It is expected that Makerspaces will continue to grow in popularity for the following reasons:
1. More people are becoming interested in making things as a creative, stress-reducing outlet.
2. An increasing availability of resources, such as 3D Printers.

3. A decreasing cost of tools and materials.
4. A desire to find new uses for recycled products.
5. The fear that AI will replace repetitive jobs.
6. More people are looking to explore their lead user innovation talents.
7. People want an escape from the virtual world and want to experience the human contacts and interest-sharing that can form in Makerspace communities.

Source: www.technavio.com/report/k-12-makerspace-materials-market-industry-analysis

Target Market:
We will start the design of our Makerspace by first determining the intended audience and range of uses, before starting to lay out the space or choose tools. We will identify the targeted age groups, educational goals, commonality of interests, and types of preferred activities, such individual creations, group projects, robotics competitions, etc.

Research Other Makerspaces:
We will check out the following national organizations and directories:

Makerspace	https://makerspace.com/
Hackerspaces	https://lists.hackerspaces.org/
Maker Faire	www.makerfaire.com
Fab Labs	www.fablabs.io
Venture Founders	
https://venturefounders.com/directory-of-maker-and-hacker-spaces/	

1. **Turn a classroom or part of the library into a Makerspace with the following types of supplies:**

Lego Building Blocks	Scrap Wooden Blocks
Plastic Fasteners	Glues and Cements
Play Doh/Clay	Paints and Brushes
Toy Parts Inventory	PVC Pipes and Fittings
Crayons and Markers	Fabric Paints
Glitter and Stars	Colorful Tapes
Hinges	Pom Poms
Cotton Balls	Popsicle Sticks
Oversized Toothpicks	Patterns, Fabrics and Threads
Jointed Action Figures	Plastic Clamps
Rubber Cooking Utensils	Construction Papers
Binder Clips	Yarn
Rubber Bands	Colored Pencils and Pens
Paperclips	Sewing Materials
Dowel Sticks	LED Lights

2. **Provide recycled materials to save money and teach about eco-friendliness:**

Recycled Copy Paper	Newspapers
Recycled Cardboard Boxes	Shoe Boxes
Scrap Wooden Blocks	Empty Egg cartons

Outdated Magazines
Pringles Tubes
Storage Containers
Scrap Textiles
Cardboard tubes from toilet paper, paper towels and wrapping paper

Tissue Boxes
Plastic Cups
Rubber Balls

3. **Provide the following types of equipment:**

Glue Guns
Safety Scissors
3D Printers
Sewing Machine
Gardening Tools
Resource: https://www.thingiverse.com/

Child Safe Hand Tools
Programmable Robots
Laser Cutters
Audio/Visual Equipment
Mannequins

4. **Organize the Makerspace with the following storage methods:**

Labeled Clear Bins
Worktables with Drawers
Shopping Baskets
Closet Space Rentals

Peg Boards
Letter Boxes
Closet Shelving

5. **Find innovative ways to fund the Makerspace:**

Launch an Afterschool Enrichment Program
Resources:
https://makerspacedir.com/listing-category/after-school-program/
Ex: https://makerspacedir.com/listing/bricks-4-kidz/
Hold Fee-based Events and Specialty Workshops
Sell merchandise, like t-shirts or hats, with our makerspace's logo.
Charge for Different Levels of Membership.
Rent out the space for birthday parties and team building events.
Secure local business donations of funds and overstock products.
Ask businesses to sponsor various programs in exchange for publicity.
Collect family recycled waste products, such as cardboard boxes.
Stage community fundraisers to raise funds and visibility.
Start a 'Maker Club' and ask the community to donate used tools.
Use a crowdfunding platform to raise money via a fundraising campaign.
Example: www.indiegogo.com
Ask the school's PTA to help raise funds and research donation sources available to teachers.
Resource: www.donorschoose.org/teachers
Apply for Research Government Grants.
Resource: https://1stmakerspace.com/grants
Source: www.edutopia.org/blog/6-strategies-funding-makerspace-paloma-garcia-lopez

6. **Use the following marketing tactics to promote Makerspace Programs:**

Create a Facebook Business Page to promote events and workshops

Launch or join a Facebook Group to share Makerspace experiences and survey results.

Resources: https://www.facebook.com/groups/makespaces/

Showcase member achievements by sharing photos and videos on Instagram and YouTube.

Collect testimonials that will stimulate word-of-mouth advertising

Design flyers about the afterschool enrichment program and hand them out to parents.

Showcase success stories at creator fairs and art exhibitions

Hold contests for the best designs.

Reach out to local media outlets with press release stories.

Hang flyers in local businesses

Purchase a mailing list to mail out postcards.

Create partnerships with local businesses to hold cross-promotions.

Set up a referral program that rewards members for recruiting new faces.

Resource:

https://desygner.com/blog/industry/how-to-market-makerspaces-business

7. **Our Makerspace teachers will serve the following roles:**

Keep the room organized and safe

Present project idea options based on storytelling

Encourage team collaborations

Teach some new skill sets to help fill knowledge gaps

Monitor and report progress

Photograph projects and forward to parents with comments

Provide support, as needed

Coach parents on how-to-play a supportive role

Organize end-of-program exhibitions and contests.

Post contest winner photos to Facebook and Instagram

Resource: www.facebook.com/groups/makerspaceteachers/

Resources:

https://www.psychologicalscience.org/observer/children-creativity-intelligence

Example: https://thelightprep.org/montessori-stream-inspired/

Supplier Sources: https://stemfinity.com/

https://gratnellslearningrooms.com/the-importance-of-makerspace/

IV. Protect Against Imitators

We will be vigilant about safeguarding our preschool business from copycats. We will focus on the following types of hard-to-imitate resources and dynamically evolve new educational philosophies, and operating and marketing strategies:
1. Keep developing proprietary technologies and processing systems that lead to productivity gains, to remain a moving target.
2. Run continuous training programs to groom and keep skilled personnel.
3. Develop a strong brand reputation based on exceptional customer service and teacher respect and trust.
4. Foster a unique organizational culture, that is, embedded in the complex processes and social relationships that exist inside the business.
5. Expand to multiple strategic locations.
6. Pursue consistent community engagement strategies, such as by helping families to support the learning process at home.
   Resource: https://blog.schoolspecialty.com/5-family-and-community-
                  engagement-strategies-to-improve-student-outcomes/
7. Reinvest profits in state-of-the-art indoor and outdoor equipment.
8. Create a unique, customizable curriculum, that can be further personalized by on student interests and talents.
9. Establish and keep open, multiple communication and progress reporting channels with parents.
10. Secure legally protected intellectual property, such as via trademarks, patents, or publishing copyrights.
11. Maintain an experimenting mindset, that will keep searching for better ways to exploit new opportunities, and remain a moving target, that is harder for competitors to get a fix on.
12. Shroud the multiple strengths in casual ambiguity, to make it harder to determine which factors are driving the advantage.
13. Incorporate other programs, such as after-school enrichment classes, party/event planning and tutoring sessions, so that the combination of offerings create a unique value proposition.
14. Establish alignment with the requirements of local elementary schools, to facilitate the ease of student transition, and prepare the student to achieve greater academic success and social development gains.
15. Form strategic partnerships, with alliance agreements, to raise the brand's visibility, and prevent imitators from forming partnerships with these valued partners.
16. Use confidentiality agreements, such as 'Non-Disclosure Agreements', to help protect trade secrets or valuable intellectual property.
17. Hold contests and exhibit the submissions that show how the preschool supports creativity, imagination development and problem-solving activities.
18. Publish articles, blogs, books and testimonials that speak to how the school has become a leader in the science of early child development.
Resources: https://learnstrategy.byu.edu/business-strategy/barriers-to-imitation
                  https://www.redpoints.com/blog/protect-your-business-from-copycats/

V. Incorporate Alternatives to Traditional Preschools

We will incorporate the following traditional alternatives to our preschool curriculum to discourage imitators, and create a unique value proposition:

1. **Homeschooling Support Services**
   We will provide support to homeschooling parents who want the flexibility to teach certain subjects at-home, in a personalized manner, and expose their children to group social development activities, at other times. We will also offer a homeschooling consultancy service for parents, and market a series or recommended curriculum-based software packages.
   Resources: www.time4learning.com/homeschool-curriculum/how-it-works/
   www.kanacademy.org

2. **Scheduled Day Drop-Off Program**
   These programs will allow parents to drop their children off at a designated facility to take some time away from childcare responsibilities. We will provide flexible scheduling options that can easily accommodate working parents and their unique needs. This program will be more affordable than traditional preschools and provide the required flexible scheduling options for busy parents.

3. **On-Line Learning/Tutoring Program**
   We will develop an online teaching platform for parents wanting to either guide their homeschooling efforts, or bridge learning gaps, by supplementing their child's education from home. We will offer educational content tailored specifically, for preschool aged children, on a subscription basis.
   Resource: www.kanacademy.org

4. **Playgroup Activities**
   We will advise parents about our daily schedule for playgroup activities, or run a daycare program that welcomes drop-ins throughout the day. We will train one teacher to be a leader of outdoor playgroup activities, and to focus on the development of fine motor skills. The desired goal will be small group learning, and encourage children to provide input and work collaboratively to play group games, and complete their shared assignments and arts and crafts projects.
   Examples: https://laurelway-playgroup.com/activities/
   https://kidscastlepreschool.com/playgroup/
   Source: https://kidscastlepreschool.com/what-is-a-playgroup-why-should-you-send-your-child-to-a-playgroup/

5. **Nature Programs**
   We will specifically design our nature programs for young children. We will offer hands-on activities, such as nature scavenger hunts, animal tracking, birdwatching, gardening, farming, beach and park cleanups, water conservation,

and nature-based crafts. We will teach the children to use things, such as leaves, flowers, twigs, or pebbles to make creative art projects. These programs will also help students to reduce stress levels, increase activity levels, improve self-confidence and promote creativity.

Source: https://naturalstart.org/resources/establishing-nature-based-preschool
            https://cleanchoiceenergy.com/news/teach-kids-about-environment
Resource: https://naturalstart.org/nature-preschools-united-states-2022-survey

6.   Dual Language Learning Programs

We will develop the expertise to teach preschoolers to become bilingual, and speak, listen, read and write in two languages, because research indicates that children who are adequately exposed to two or more languages at an early age can make significant progress.

Resource: www.duolingo.com
Directory: https://mommypoppins.com/miami-south-florida-kids/preschools/
            bilingual-language-immersion-preschools-in-south-florida

7.   Summer Camp Program

This program will deliver a blend of education and fun, ensuring an enriching experience. Students will engage in arts, crafts, STEM labs, and science experiments. We will also offer movie days and fitness activities to keep the campers active and entertained.

Example: www.tanglewoodacademy.com/programs/summer-camp/

8.   Afterschool Enrichment Programs

We will develop afterschool enrichment programs that will welcome homeschooled children and students from other local preschools. Examples of these learn-by-doing classes will include: cooking classes, Lego building, song and dance lessons, fitness training, and technology workshops.

9.   Makerspace Afterschool Enrichment Program

We will create a collaborative work space inside our school library for making, learning, exploring and sharing learn-by-doing experiences, that use low tech to no tech tools for preschool students. We will turn one room in our preschool into a 'Makerspace', that children will use to improve their creative intelligence. Refer to how to 'Build a Makerspace Room, in Section 2. We will end the program by holding an art exhibition, featuring the completed projects, and award prizes to contest winners.

Resource:
Maker State   https://maker-state.com/programs/start-an-afterschool-makerspace/
A national STEM-mastery after-school and camps program.

10.   Builder Birthday Parties

We will develop a new revenue stream by turning birthday celebrations into learning, builder birthday parties in our own 'Makerspace'. Our party services will include: trained instructors, take home builder projects, Lego block building,

building art drawing classes, telescope making, bracelets designing with LED lights, robot-shaped cupcakes, pizza and healthy beverages, custom party invitations, gift thank you cards, and goody bags with unique. handcrafted party favors.　Example:　https://builderbirthdays.com/

11.　Children with Special Needs Programs
We will develop a curriculum for children with special needs. This special education program will ensure that students with learning disabilities receive specialized instruction, that is, designed to meet their unique learning needs. We will make certain to provide students with written copies of orally presented lectures.

Resources:

Positive Action　　　www.positiveaction.net/blog/teaching-special-education-strategies

It provides a research-based SPED curriculum that works with students who receive special education of all types, including: Autism, Down syndrome, ADD/ADHD, Learning disabilities, Emotional disturbance, and Physical and intellectual disabilities

Source:　　　www.graduateprogram.org/2022/11/strategies-for-teaching-students-with-disabilities/

https://ws.edu/student-services/disability/teaching/learning/index.aspx

www.smartproductivemom.com/alternatives-to-preschool/

VI. Develop New Revenue Streams

Conduct Parenting Workshops

We will organize monthly workshops that help to build parenting skills, which are foundational to a child's educational and social development success. Our objective will to strengthen the parent-child connection and our place in the community. We will develop a parent workshop series registration form to help collect important data for future growth strategies. Parents can decide if they want to sign-up for individual workshops or register for the complete, discounted 'Preschool Parenting Training Program'. We will promote these workshops via our website, e-newsletter, flyers, event posting sites, referral discount coupons, and social media ads. We will turn these workshops into informative social gatherings by featuring presentations from local childhood development experts, from local practices and colleges, holding door prize contests, and the serving of beverages and snacks. We will end workshops by handing out satisfaction surveys that ask for comments and improvement suggestions.

Examples:
https://shop.incredibleyears.com/products/preschool-basic-parenting-training-program
https://www.lernerchilddevelopment.com/parent-workshops

Parenting workshops will cover the following types of topics:

1.	Child Discipline	2.	Nutrition Guidance
3.	Problem-solving	4.	Learning styles
5.	Communication skills	6.	Family relationships
7	Language development	8.	Self-confidence
9.	Single parenting	10.	Critical thinking
11.	Burnout Prevention/Solutions	12.	Anger management
13.	Technology balancing/choices	14.	Empathy skills
15.	Parenting preparations	16.	Curriculum previews
17.	Encouraging Story Talk	18.	Fine Motor Skills Development
19.	Active Learning Techniques	20.	Potty Training
21.	Reading Skills Development	22.	Good Sleep Habits
23.	Handling Tantrums	24.	Stopping Biting

Examples:
Early Childhood Adventures   https://earlychildhoodadventures.net/parent-and-me/
They partnered with Parent Collaborative to house monthly parenting workshops for all enrolled families. This is a requirement for all Preschool Families enrolled and is optional for VPK Families. Their program philosophy embraces the crucial role that families play in the education of their children.

Pricing:
$____ (175?) for two family members of an enrolled student
$____ (200?) for outside participants per person.
$____ (25?) discount coupons for referrals.

Distribute Workshop Manuals
We will also assemble all of the content and questions posed at the above workshops and turn the bound materials into a for-sale series of books. We will also form affiliate marketing sales relationships with book retailers, such as Amazon Associates Affiliate Marketing Program (https://affiliate-program.amazon.com/). To earn sales commissions, of about 10 percent, we will need to develop a qualifying website or mobile app.
Examples:
Highscope.org/product/bringing-active-learning-home-workshops-for-preschool-parents/
www.loveandlogic.com/collections/parents

Offer Parent-directed Online Courses and Webinars
These presenters will blend story-telling with highly effective parenting solutions, to meet the challenges facing today's parents. These programs will include an online parent workbook, videos, exercises, downloadable tip sheets, emails, podcasts and optional text reminders. They will be ideal for geographically isolated parents, or are too busy to attend face-to-face sessions.

Popular Workshop Titles:
How to Gain Respects from Your Children
How to Increase Family Cooperation and Team Spirit

How to Manage Toddler Tantrums
How to Solve Hitting and Biting Behavioral Problems
How to Achieve Potty Training Success
How to Stop the Mimicking of Bad Behaviors

Examples:
https://www.goodinside.com/workshops/
https://www.triplep.net/glo-en/triple-p-online-webinar/
https://www.loveandlogic.com/collections/classes-and-conferences

Offer Newsletter Subscriptions
We will publish a monthly newsletter with the content from our workshops and webinars. We will make the monthly newsletter free to enrolled student families, and charge a fee to non-member subscribers.

Newsletter Content Ideas:
Community At-Large:

Business Coupons	Sponsorship Ads and Notices
Public Events Calendar	Community Education-related News

Preschool:

Lunch and Snack Menus	Healthy Menu Suggestions
Parent Reminders	Monthly Lesson Plans
School Policy Changes	Links to Social Media/Blogs
New Family Welcomes	Child Photos Doing Projects
Student Milestones	Teacher/Preschool Milestones
School Events Calendar	Parent Testimonials
Child Raising Insights	

Template Resources: www.canva.com/newsletters/templates/preschool/
                             www.2care2teach4kids.com/newsletters.html
Platform Resources:
Patreon   www.patreon.com
An online crowdfunding membership platform that can collect recurring payments to support a creator.
Substack   www.substack.com
A website providing a user-friendly platform for writers and journalists, allowing creators to share their work and directly monetize it.
Directory: https://www.mightynetworks.com/resources/patreon-alternatives

Parent Coaching
We will observe the child in their natural settings, either at home and/or school, and evaluate how they function in real-life environments, and coach parents about how to best support them. The fee will be $ _____ (200.00?) for a 45-minute session. We will offer multiple consult packages at discounted rates. We will make use of the telehealth platform, as the basis for interacting with parents.

Example: https://www.simplepractice.com/
Directory: https://medtechfounder.com/best-telemedicine-platforms/
Examples: https://www.lernerchilddevelopment.com/parent-coaching
               https://www.lernerchilddevelopment.com/parent-consultation

Transportation Services

We plan to offer directly, or form a partnership, with a fee-based transportation service. We will offer safe and reliable transportation, to and from school. We will provide transportation services for field trips, and to and from a variety of extracurricular activities, including aftercare programs, sports practices, athletic trips, or sports events, music lessons, etc. We will also expand into private transportation services for families, such as transportation to events, appointments, airport shuttles, cruise ports, and other destinations.
Examples: https://www.smartkidstransportation.com/
               https://www.kidsride2school.com/

After-school and Weekend Child Enrichment Programs

We will help preschool children to cultivate new, extra or real-life skills. Children will be able to choose to take up any new hobby based on their interests. The objective of these enrichment activities will be to:
1.   Encourage problem-solving skills and critical thinking by the attendees.
2.   Keep children positively occupied in the latter part of the day.
3.   Generate a better return on the investment in school facilities.
4.   Make the preschool visible to a wider audience.
5.   Create new revenue streams.

Best Practices:

Parents will have the option to pay in full upfront a discounted amount or choose convenient monthly installments. When not in class, students can complete homework assignments, or enjoy a snack in our designated After School Room. For the safety and security of our students, parents must go to the After School Room entrance to sign out their children during pick-up, with a preschool-issued dismissal card or a government-issued ID, for relative listed verification purposes. For a separate transport fee, we will pick-up children from other selected locations and bring them to our afterschool enrichment programs.
Model Programs: http://www.songanddanceinc.com/after-school-program.html
                    https://www.salvationarmyusa.org/usn/teach-kids/

We plan to offer a rotating schedule of once-a-week, enrichment classes for children, by developing the following types of programs:

Gymnastics	Arts and Crafts
Cooking/Baking	Music Lessons
Lego Building	Yoga
Dance Classes	Martial Arts
Acting	Singing
Coding/Programming	Robotics

Language Learning	Board Games
Math Skills	Seed Planting
Sports	STEM
Reading	Creative Writing
Swimming	Recycling Crafts
Drama Club	Baby/Toddler Ballet Classes
Mommy and Me Classes	Baby/Toddler Yoga Classes
Technology Learning	Robotics

Resources: www.jetlearn.com/blog/after-school-enrichment-activities
www.idtech.com/blog/ultimate-list-of-after-school-enrichment-activities

Baby and Toddler Ballet Classes

These ballet classes will allow caregivers to have intense bonding time with their child, and to create memories that will last a lifetime. They will also give the school the opportunity for more visibility within the community and increased preschool enrollment exposure, and to benefit financially from supply sales and the holding of end-of-program recitals. These classes will benefit from the school's existing parking lot, sound system, and student lockers.

Source: https://babyballet.co.uk/shop/
Example: https://www.babyballetlongisland.com/
https://www.cdcdance.com/baby-ballerina
Directory: www.mindbodyonline.com/explore/fitness/classes/baby-ballet-miami-shores-ayala-royal-ballet-overtown

Baby and Toddler Yoga Classes

We will offer yoga classes that to early age children that encourages self-esteem and body awareness, and is a physical activity that is noncompetitive and noncombative. Teaching toddlers the practice of Yoga, at these young ages, will help children to develop lifelong healthy habits that will be sustained long-term. Additionally, yoga classes will promote concentration and a sense of calmness and relaxation. Additional equipment requirements may only be exercise-mats and a music system. We will also profit from the sales of vending machine snacks and beverages.
Resources: https://yogafactoryfitness.com/kids-yoga-classes/
https://www.montessoriinreallife.com/home/tag/toddler+yoga

Recycle DIY Crafts Afterschool Program

This program will involve the turning the contents of a recycle bin into a craft supply store. This after-school enrichment program will provide the following benefits:
1.   Become a differentiating source of new afterschool revenues.
2.   Generate newsworthy press release coverage.
3.   Make constructive use of recyclables to help save the planet.
4.   Inspire creativity in the student attendees.
5.   Realize higher profit margins due to the lower cost of supplies.

Examples: Turn plastic bottles into planers, birdfeeders and piggy banks.
               Tin cans into storage containers, lanterns and pencil holders
               Cardboard boxes into dollhouses
Resources:
https://www.weareteachers.com/earth-day-crafts-classroom-activities/
https://modpodgerocksblog.com/recycled-crafts-for-kids/
https://www.pinterest.com/housingaforest/recycle/

Lego Block and Robot Building Program
The objective will be to provide a Lego preschool fine motor skills activity that will also help improve children's skills and creativity. Children will be inspired to create a robot that reflects their unique personality and interests, with speech, songs, sounds, lights, movements and interactions. We will feature the LEGO Education Spike Prime Program because it offers bright colors, kid-friendly designs and drag-and-drop coding tools.

Example: https://mightykidsacademy.com/learn-with-lego-preschool-fine-motor-
                  skills-activity/
Source: https://www.lego.com/en-us/categories/robots-for-kids
                 https://education.lego.com/en-us/
                 www.preschoolplayandlearn.com/learning-with-legos-for-preschoolers/
Resources:
Lego Mindstorms   www.lego.com/en-us/themes/mindstorms
These are toolkits that allow students to make programmable robots.
First Robotics   www.firstinspires.org/robotics/frc

Technology Learning Program
We will give these program attendees the opportunity to test out daily lessons with real-world, hands-on applications. We will teach children to explore touch screens loaded with a wide variety of developmentally appropriate interactive media experiences. We will also incorporate technology into program lessons by encouraging our students to play educational games and solve puzzles on the computer and iPad. With technology becoming a main focus in Elementary Schools, the objective will be for children to develop a sense of comfort and ease with new discovery and interactive learning methods, and smart TVs, search engines, computers and mobile devices, at an early age. We will co-create digital storytelling books, with photos of the children's play or work. We will also require continuous interaction with the teachers to prevent student feelings of isolation and loneliness.
Resources: www.naeyc.org/resources/topics/technology-and-media/preschoolers-and-
                kindergartners
Source: www.twinscience.com/en/parent-advice/benefits-of-technology-to-children/

Coding Workshops
Research indicates that learning coding at an early age (3 years and up) is becoming a priority for parents and teacher because it can improve mathematical conceptualization. Young children will learn basic coding principles through a drag-and-drop icon-based interface. We will make it a game and incorporate different hands-on toys to engage

children in learning the steps to thinking like a programmer. We will also offer a combination of online and classroom-based preschool coding classes.

Source: www.learning.com/blog/teaching-children-coding-ages-3-and-up/
Example: https://www.nowtechacademy.com/stem-preschool
                    https://outschool.com/online-classes/grades/preschool-pdl-coding
Directory: https://techbootcamps.utexas.edu/blog/coding-books-for-kids/
                    https://stackoverflow.blog/2021/01/12/want-to-teach-your-kids-to-code-here-are-three-apps-that-can-help/
Resource:

Little Red Coding Club   www.twinkl.com/apps/research-little-red-coding-club
It fosters playful learning and early coding skills and knowledge when used by young children (4-6).
Make Wonder   https://www.makewonder.com/en/
Provides pre-built lessons and activities to make teaching coding easier than ever.

Drama Club Afterschool Program

The purpose of the drama club will be to engage students in the performing arts and theater. Students will learn acting, singing, dancing and communication skills, work on building sets and making props, design costumes and makeup, and promote the sales of event tickets. The preschool will not only benefit from student enrollment fees, but also from the sales of supplies and performance event tickets. The program will not only boost the self-confidence of the attendees, but also ready them for the end-of-school graduation performance ceremonies.

Resources:
https://scienceandliteracy.org/how-to-start-a-drama-club-in-elementary-school/
https://www.dramanotebook.com/teach-drama-class/

Song and Dance Afterschool Program

Research indicates that toddler dance classes take off beginning age three. At that time, kids are receptive to social cues, the concept of play, movement, and cognitive thinking skills, which can all appear within the context of a fun experience. Our program will be designed to provide children with the chance for self-expression and to build their self-confidence. We will feature dance lessons as a physical exercise that improves coordination, creativity, and motor and muscle skills. Dancing will pose the opportunity for children to be more social with each other. Students will be able to choose from jazz, tap, hip hop, ballet, musical theater, and choir classes. Ideally, these students will get the chance to exhibit these new performance skills at our graduation ceremonies and other community events.

Resource: https://ocmusicdance.org/blog/the-value-of-music-and-dance-in-your-preschoolers-life
Example: https://www.mothergoosetime.com/dance-and-fitness/

In our marketing materials, we will promote the following program benefits:
      Builds self-confidence   Enables self-expression

<table>
<tr><td>Develops language skills</td><td>Improves communication skills</td></tr>
<tr><td>Fosters physical skills</td><td>Develops creativity and imagination</td></tr>
<tr><td>Improves memory skills</td><td></td></tr>
</table>

Source: www.bukitsunriseschool.com/single-post/the-importance-of-singing-and-dancing-for-preschoolers

Model Program: http://www.broadwaykidsstudio.com/after-school/
Resource: www.pinterest.com/pin/playlist-10-songs-to-get-preschoolers-moving-and-dancing-teach-preschool-music--292945150774333393/

Virtual Tutoring Programs

We will develop virtual tutoring programs, via the internet, because they can provide students and families with more personalized, affordable and unlimited options, regardless of their geography. These virtual classes will be more convenient for both parents and children. These online programs will require a Zoom Account (https://zoom.us/signup#/signup), Google Classroom (https://sites.google.com/view/classroom-workspace/) and a learning portal, such as Thinkific.com. We will ask for feedback from participants to improve the engagement experience. We will use the Breakout Room function to assign students to groups.

Equipment List:

Writing Tablet	Document Camera
Headphones	Laptop
Microphone	Webcam
Solid Background	

Platform Directories: https://outschool.com/online-classes/preschool-tutoring
https://www.wyzant.com/Florida_preschool_tutors.aspx
www.learnworlds.com/online-learning-platforms/
www.splashlearn.com/blog/best-tutoring-websites/
Resources: https://www.create-learn.us/blog/after-school-enrichment-activities/
www.create-learn.us/blog/coding-platforms-for-kids/
www.learnit.com
Afterschool Programs: www.prodigygame.com/main-en/blog/after-school-programs/
www.romper.com/parenting/virtual-after-school-programs

Online English Learning

We will establish an online English Learning Platform to generate another revenue stream. Through gamified interactive live lessons, children will learn English, while having fun. Live lessons will be conducted through our interactive live lesson system.

Directory:
https://browncowenglish.com/five-child-friendly-websites-to-help-you-learn-english/

Examples:

Cambly	https://www.cambly.com/kids
Online Kids Academy	www.onlinekidsacademy.com/
VIP Kid	www.vipkid.com/mkt/faq/becoming-teacher
Pear Deck Learning	www.peardeck.com

An interactive presentation and lesson delivery tool that can be used via the web or as an add-on or integration with a variety of other programs. Students join teachers' Pear Deck sessions with codes and then use their devices to follow along with the teacher's slideshow on a classroom screen.

Foreign Language Learning

We will develop programs to boost children's foreign language learning skills, because children are natural pronunciation imitators and language acquirers. They are self-motivated to pick up language without conscious learning, unlike adolescents and adults, and have less of a fear of saying something wrong. We will encourage children to watch movies, play, sing and read in both their first and second languages.
Resources:

| Mindsnacks | https://elevateapp.com/ |

Offers audio clips, games and lessons to help learn foreign languages.

| Rosette Stone for Students | https://www.rosettastone.com/students/ |

Children Entertainment Events

We plan to co-sponsor fee-based children's entertainment events with local businesses. The events will have specific, age-appropriate purposes and themes. Event examples will include puppet shows, magic shows, theatrical plays, or cartoon films, which will be provided on Saturday mornings. We will also consider juggler and pantomime performances, scavenger hunts, dance parties, video game tournaments, and water painting contests. The parents will be able to drop-off their children on Saturday mornings. We will provide child-oriented and approved entertainment, and lunch for an all-inclusive fee. These events will conclude with a discussion of the just viewed session. We will promote these events with flyers, e-newsletter coupons, open house rehearsal previews, press releases, and social media postings. We will also list these entertainment events and summer camps on Eventbrite.com, allevents.in/, and Ticketsource.us.

Examples:	www.eventbrite.com/d/fl--miramar/kids/
	https://allevents.in/miramar-fl/kids#
Resources:	https://hub.theeventplannerexpo.com/entertainment/7-kid-friendly-event-entertainment-ideas-for-social-celebrations
	www.ticketsource.us/blog/how-to-plan-a-family-friendly-event

VII.   Market Curriculum Materials

Curriculum Book Sales
These books will cover curriculums, learning activities, and education philosophies from different preschool teaching disciplines, for both in-school and at-home environments.

Examples: www.amazon.com/The-Highscope-Preschool-Curriculum/dp/1573796506
                 www.amazon.com/XXL-Montessori-Preschool-Workbook-Kindergarten/
                 www.amazon.com/Working-Reggio-Way-Beginners-American/

Curriculum Materials and Supplies
We will sell our lesson plans, assessments, review packs, and project guides. Our curriculum bundle will also contain letter charts, alphabet worksheets, and games for every letter of the alphabet.
Examples: https://craftyclassroom.com/product/preschool-bundle/
                             https://shop.pathsprogram.com/collections/pkk-components
Resources:
Teachers Pay Teachers   www.teacherspayteachers.com
A marketplace where teachers offer their original curricular materials to other educators. The sire is searchable by grade level, subject, price and resource type.

Teachers Notebook   https://company.overdrive.com/2014/03/03/overdrive-acquires-
                     popular-marketplace-for-k-12-educational-materials/

Curriculum Kits
A wide range of tools and materials will be assembled and offered in these kits to support and encourage children's natural curiosity tendencies, and the desire to pursue fun activities and in-depth investigations.
Examples:
https://learningboxpreschool.com/
www.kaplanco.com/product/63054/investigations-kit-for-preschool?c=25|CU1070

Publish Preschool Branded How-to Booklets
We plan to create and publish a series of how-to-learn booklets, with covers that reference the location of and contact options for our preschool. The booklets will also contain the resumes of the teachers who contribute articles and other content. These booklets will also provide an annotated list of recommended books for children at different age levels. Similar pamphlets will focus on selecting children's toys, designing children's rooms, engaging in creative play, and/or solutions for dealing with behavioral and nutritional problems. These booklets, imprinted with our logo and contact information, will be advertised in the local paper or over the radio, or with flyers distributed widely through pediatricians, churches, libraries, and service clubs. We will also set up a booklet for-sale library in the reception area of our preschool. We plan to expand our line of educational video tutorials and workbook products, as a source of holiday gift items.

Example: https://kdp.amazon.com/en_US/help/topic/G200735480
Resources: https://kindlepreneur.com/how-to-publish-childrens-book/
Directory: https://kindlepreneur.com/best-self-publishing-companies/

VIII.   Home Party Plan Sales of Educational Games

We will use commissioned sales consultants to organize and manage these home sales parties. The party host will earn free educational products and be able to buy other products at half price, based on party sales. The parties will be conducted online, via Zoom (https://zoom.us/), or in person. Once we have scheduled our Zoom event, we will get a link that we can send to our guests. We will make available sample products to demonstrate at the party, and play a YouTube video tutorial about the usage and benefits of our complete line of products. We will use a software program to invite friends of the host to the party and email or text reminders the day before the scheduled party event. These products will also be available for sale on our website. We will make available healthy snacks and beverages at these sales parties. All attendees will also receive a giveaway premium with our imprinted logo.

Source: https://directsalesinspiration.com/zoom-parties/
               https://partywizz.com/blog/general/planning-a-zoom-party/
               https://freelancemvp.com/how-to-sell-on-zoom/
Resources:
Epixel MLM Software   www.epixelmlmsoftware.com/party-plan-mlm-software
This software has the following modules: host training program, party calendar, compensation calculator, payout compressions and consultant/host profiles.

Infinite MLM Software   https://infinitemlmsoftware.com/party-plan-mlm-software.php
Distributors are given practical tools and reports for overseeing and assisting their party hosts, which promotes their success and motivation.

Examples:
Raise Smart Kid   www.raisesmartkid.com/educational-toys-and-gifts
Discovery Toys   www.discoverytoys.us/pages/host-a-party
Simply Fun   https://simplyfun.com/
Turtle Diary   www.turtlediary.com/games/preschool.html

Wondertree   https://www.wondertree.co/pricing/
Their games are designed for children with moderate challenges in areas, such as motor skills, cognition and educational needs. They incorporate gamification by using Augmented Reality technology to make therapy more enjoyable for children. WonderTree detects real world surroundings and overlays virtual environments on top of it to create a fun approach to physiotherapy.

Develop Affiliate Relationships

We will pursue an affiliate relationship with Amazon.com, which has the largest affiliate program in the world. Amazon pays 4% to 8% in commission to its affiliates. We will send people to buy specific items on Amazon using our referral link to receive a commission on. For example, at holiday times, we will create a "Parents Gift Shopping List" of books and educational toys. Parents will click on the assigned special referral link to go shop. Anything they put in their cart during that session you receive commission on. Other child-focused products, that are offered on a monthly subscription basis, and have affiliate programs, include Little Passports, Surprise Ride, and BabbaBox.

Source: www.naeyc.org/resources/blog/building-reciprocal-relationships

Other Resources:
Clickbank   https://www.clickbank.com/
Provides high-converting affiliate offers, reliable tracking, on-time payments, and industry-leading education.

IX.   Collect More Itemized Fees

We will try not to abuse or upset parents by collecting too many fees. We will give detailed explanations, as to why the required fees are being levied. We will also advise parents that if they assist with fundraising drives, we may be able to offset certain fees.

We will increase revenues by charging a mix of the following common fees:

1.	Registration Fee	2.	Late Payment Fees
3.	Early Drop-off Fees	4.	Late Pickup Fees
5.	Early Drop-off/ Late Pickup Fees	6.	Annual Supplies Fees
7.	Technology Usage Fees	8.	Security Fee
9.	Maintenance Fee	10.	Field Trip Fees
11.	Graduation Ticket Fees	12.	Graduation Gown Rental Fees
13.	Uniform Fees	14.	Transportation Fees
15.	Organic Meal Fees	16.	Optional Special Activities
17.	Remote Camera Viewing Fees	18.	Annual Supplies Fee
19.	Extra Class Fees	20.	Personalized Curriculum Fees
21.	Weekend Daycare Fees	22.	ACH Processing Fees
23.	Technology Fee	24.	Return Check Fee
25.	Withdrawal Without Notice Fee	26.	Accreditation Fees
27.	Capital Improvement Fee	28.	Waiting List Fee
29.	Re-enrolling Enrollment Fees	30.	New Student Enrollment Fees
31.	Healthy Snack Fees		

Example: https://www.welbourneavenuenursery.org/fee-schedule

X.   Multi-Purpose or Sublease Extra Facility Rooms

Preschool Room Rentals
Our plan is to monetize the weekends and weekday evenings when our facility is not being used or is sitting empty. Because of the time-consuming set-up and cleanup of at-home birthday parties, more parents are choosing to host their parties at venues. According to IAAPA, these venues see average revenue of nearly $400 per party. As a side hustle, we will rent out an unused room in our preschool for children's parties, because many people do not also have the space for larger gatherings, and are ready to rent affordable and conveniently located spaces. We will either rent our place as is, or team with a company that will provide chairs, tables, and other party gear rentals. We will promote these room rentals with flyers, e-newsletter articles, website blog, Yelp, Facebook Ads, Craigslist and Peerspace.com. We will promote the rental of the room for birthday parties by writing articles entitled: "Special Birthday Party Ideas to Captivate Toddlers." We may also add an external entrance to the room, to maintain its separate, secure access, from the preschool after hours. We will also consider hiring or forming an alliance with a birthday party planner and manager, and create a program with a shared revenue model. We will also promote the rental of the space for co-working space rentals, photo shoots and as a classroom for a child tutoring or cooking school business.

Example: https://giggster.com/listing/preschool-space-for-rent
Booking Locations: www.splacer.com
                    www.Giggster.com
                    www.peerspace.com
                    www.spacefy.com
                    www.eventective.com/USA
                    www.thestorefront.com

Birthday Party Room
We will enter the children's birthday party business as a flexible and affordable venue rental space, because parents, with any degree of surplus income, and social-media pressures, are wanting to create the perfect, status-conferring, private, child birthday celebrations, for their cherished loved ones.

We will designate one room within the preschool as a combination recreational activities and birthday party room. We will make this change for the following reasons:
1.   To create a distinctive attraction to increase child-driven demand for the preschool from their parents.
2.   To hold birthday parties to generate a secondary revenue stream.

3.   To increase the preschool exposure by welcoming non-student, birthday party attendees.

The birthday parties will also offer affiliate marketing or brokering commissions from the following types of product suppliers and service providers:

Balloon Artists	Makeup Artists/Face Painters
Magicians	Children's Party Planner
Caterers	DJs
Bakeries	Party Decorators
Mobile Princess Spa	Arts and Crafts Instructors
Dance Instructors	Craft Suppliers
Fabric Painting	Birdhouse Painting
Cake Decorating Instructors	Favors or Goodie Gift Bags
Photographer/Videographer	Costume Rentals
Party Equipment Rentals	Cleaners
Bounce House Rentals	Professional Clowns
Party Planners	Ball Pits

Key Birthday Party Room Design Elements:
1.   Happy Birthday photo background and signage, with preschool name.
2.   Interactive games: air hockey, ping pong, billiards, basketball hoops, magnetic darts, cornhole, ring toss, Junga, video games, etc.
3.   Eating tables and bean bag seating for birthday attendees.
4.   Food warming and serving buffet and snack table.
5.   Project building work tables
6.   Indoor playground offers a wide range of play structures, including slides, oversized doll houses, train tables, remote control car racetrack, and climbing walls, to encourage imaginative play.

Example:	https://www.fandory.com/birthday-parties
Source:	www.pinterest.com/evelynsobrino/children-party-decor-ideas/
	https://www.lemonthistle.com/affordable-kids-birthday-party-decor/
	https://www.preschool-plan-it.com/preschool-birthday-party.html
Resources:	www.amazon.com/Birthday-Party-Decorations-Kids/s?k= Birthday+Party+Decorations+for+Kids

Develop Play Café Room
We will turn one of the preschool rooms into a play café room for the following purposes:
1.   Rent to families to hold birthday parties.
2.   Open to the public on weekends as a recreational center for toddlers to generate ticket sales and enhance preschool visibility.
3.   Give one-hour access to preschool students, during the school day, to foster social and motor skills development.
4.   Flag as a competitive advantage in all marketing materials.

Develop Party Planner App

We will develop an online booking and party planner App that features the birthday party agreement with parents: assigning responsibilities, establishing reservation dates and times, number of attendees, party theme, food supplier/menu, party support requirements, parent name, contact information, cancellation policy, and related costs and payment terms. It will also design birthday invitations and enable parents to email or text prospective party attendees, and remind them of the coming event. We will also seek permission to stay in contact with these possible future preschool students.

Examples: www.signnow.com/features/recommend-birthday-party-contract-template-
                template-electronically-sign
                https://www.pandadoc.com/birthday-party-contract-template/
Resources: https://www.evite.com/
                https://www.punchbowl.com/
                https://play.google.com/store/apps/details?id=com.birthday.
                birthdayinvitation&hl=en_US&gl=US
Directory: https://www.planningpod.com/party-planning-software.cfm

Children's Party Franchise

We will develop the expertise to franchise our children's party operations model.
Example: https://www.pumpitupparty.com/franchise-opportunities/
Directory: https://americasbestfranchises.com/find-franchises/search/childrens-
                birthday-party/

Children's Event/Party Planning Service

We will offer a children's party planning service because in today's fast-paced and busy world, with dual income providers, a lot of parents lack the time to sit down and make preparations for their children's upcoming parties themselves, and must choose to hire professional party planners to do the job. By offering this service, in conjunction with our room rental business, we will be able to offer more of an inclusive package deal. We will also create a list of supplier contacts or pre-approved service providers.
Source: www.streetdirectory.com/travel_guide/192493/money_management/
                earning_money_as_a_childrens_party_planner.html

Co-working Desk Space Rental Room

We will make it convenient for parents to drop-off their children for preschool and then go to the next on-premises door to rent a soundproofed, co-working desk space. Parents will be able to rent space by the hour, day, week or month, and possibly have a window view of the preschool's facility.
Resource: www.liquidspace.com
Examples:
Tiny Beans   https://tinybeans.com/co-working-spaces-that-offer-child-care/
Wiggle and Work   https://wiggleandwork.com/

Studio Photography Rental Room

We will create a quick setup, multi-purpose room, as a photography studio, to generate significant revenues from the taking of holiday family photos, birthday photos and graduation photos. Research indicates that a 10 x 15 feet room is a minimum recommended length/width of the room for a studio. We will start with a key light, a fill light, and a backlight, lighting modifiers (umbrellas), light stands, digital camera, 50 mm and 85 mm prime lenses, lens filters, tripod, props, and several backdrop options.
Resource: https://www.tagvenue.com/blog/setting-up-a-photography-studio/

New/Used Children's Book Sales from Library Room

Research indicates that children who have been exposed to library preschool programs showed a greater number of emergent literacy behaviors, and pre-reading skills than those in a control group.
Source: https://pambarnhill.com/library-for-preschoolers/
                   https://playtolearnpreschool.us/library-dramatic-play-center/
                   https://www.scholastic.com/teachers/teaching-tools/book-lists/15-must-have-books-for-your-prek-classroom-library.html

We will create a separate, secure, reading/library/retailing room, in our preschool, by building bookcases, and a flexible, circular seating arrangement. We will offer for-sale new and used books, that we will obtain on a consignment basis. We will also enable secure, direct, exterior access to the reading/library/book sales room, to extend the selling hours beyond the preschool open hours on weekends and evenings. We will source some of the used book inventory from local families, garage sales, yard sales, estate sales, library clearance sales, and thrift stores. We will also use this combination preschool library and retail bookselling space to feature storybooks, educational toys and games, puppets, stuffed animals, and comic books and puzzles.
Resource:
Book Scouter   www.bookscouter.com
Design Resource: https://childcarelounge.com/pages/preschool-library-area-book-nook-quiet-corner
                      www.scholastic.com/teachers/teaching-tools/articles/6-tips-to-help-set-up-a-classroom-library.html

Puppet Theater Shows

We will use a section of our on-site library to build a mobile puppet stage, and sell tickets to both in-person and online puppet show theater events. These shows will be targeted to children between the ages of 3 to 5, because they really respond to this type of live theater, multi-sensory experience. The shows will be free for enrolled students, and non-members will be charged a nominal fee. In both cases, we will benefit from the added exposure or visibility resulting from the shows, and the listing of the puppet theater as a competitive advantage for our preschool, in our marketing materials. We will also offer group discounts for families who also want to rent the space to hold birthday parties.
Source: https://best-start.org/blog/the-amazing-benefits-of-playing-with-puppets-in-early-childhood-
Example;   https://puppet.org/visit/buy-tickets/

Vending Machine Sales

We will explore this passive income method, and designate an area to setup vending machines that dispense healthy snacks and beverages to students, teachers and parents. We will feature packaged organic fruits and veggies, dried fruits, veggie chips, trail mix, gourmet popcorn, and granola, water bottles, and energy bars. We will purchase these items in bulk from a food distributor and re-stock the machines ourselves. This designated area will contain a select number of tables and chairs, counter space, napkin dispensers, and waste bins.

Resources: www.healthyyouvending.com/
                https://www.etsy.com/market/kids_vending_machines
Examples: https://www.tiktok.com/discover/daycare-vending-machine
Source: www.vendinglocator.com/blog/cash-in-on-the-trend-18-must-have-
                healthy-vending-machine-snacks
                www.vendinglocator.com/blog/vending-machines-in-schools-both-
                favorable-and-profitable

Daycare Services Room

We will setup one room to be able to offer a basic daycare service to parents that are more budget focused. The focus will be on stocking the room with safe toys and games, and the management of organized children's playgroups. We will separate the space into different interest areas, such as a block construction corner, a symbolic play corner, manipulative corner, and child sanctuary/literacy library. We will use rugs and shelving or storage units to separate the spaces in the room. We will soft music and low lighting to help set the very important sleepy-time nap mood. We will build-in the capacity to handle emergency drop-offs. The prime target market will be local working mothers.

Examples: www.pinterest.com/pin/inspiring-daycare-room-setup-ideas--
                366128644718734752/
Resource: www.biggerpockets.com/forums/32/topics/172318-daycare-center-how-
                do-i-market-it-price-it-lease-it-etc

On-Demand Drop-in Activity Center

Children will be able to participate in free play, educational learning opportunities, age-appropriate games and activities, and social development experiences. Parents can drop-off their children at any time and pay by the hour, with no contract or time commitments. We will also offer a membership program, whereby parents can sign-up for allocated hour determined packages. Discounts will be awarded based on the number of children and number of care hours selected in the package deal. Discounts will also be given to families who have children actively enrolled in our preschool program. Members will also qualify for 'Parent's Night Out' discounted rates.

Example: https://thestopandplay.com/membership/
Directory: www.winnie.com
Example: https://winnie.com/miramar/drop-in-daycares

Hopping In   https://hoppingin.com/daycares-using-hopping/

With the HoppingIn service, parents can book daycare on demand with member childcare businesses. They can browse daycare availability and book the spot they need. Parents can select half-days or full days, and reserve them up to a month in advance. If there is no vacancy, they can be added to a waitlist and be advised as soon as the spot is available.

XI.   Personalized Learning Programs

These customized programs will be driven by the following considerations:
1. Some parents like the status associated with choosing the best, top-of-the-line program for their child.
2. Customized learning requires teachers guiding students on their individualized social development and immersive learning journeys, and is based on each student's abilities, strengths, needs, skills, and interests.
3. Individualized learning plans will be based on the individual student's starting knowledge base, or what they know, known interests, and collaborations to uncover how the child learns best.
4. Students are given differentiated instruction based on their personal learning profiles and characteristics.
5. Teachers will closely monitor each student in the personalized program, and provide extra guidance and support, as needed.
6. Teachers will be trained and empowered to allocate more time for small, personalized group instruction, when needed by students.
7. State-of-the-art, educational technologies will be used to connect with and engage students in advanced personalized learning programs.
8. Classrooms will feature flexible seating and workstation arrangements, and the aesthetically chosen room décor will inspire curiosity and creativity.
9. Students will be given the ability to re-watch recorded lessons and online programs, at home, with parental guidance and support.
10. Student will engage in more group activities, together during class, so these students can have their personalized lessons re-enforced, from a collaborative and different perspective.

Resources:
www.understood.org/en/articles/personalized-learning-what-you-need-to-know
www.prodigygame.com/main-en/blog/personalized-learning/

Facilitate Student-centered Learning
We will facilitate student-centered learning because it is designed to place the needs and interests of individual students at the forefront of the educational process, to create a customized and self-directed learning experience. We will promote the following four main characteristics of a student-centered learning model:
1. Listening to the voices of students as they express their needs and interests.
2. Enabling student choice controls over the pace of their learning and pathways.
3. Facilitating collaboration between small groups of students to accomplish shared tasks.

4.   Advancing based on a proven sense of competency.
5.   Continuing to monitor student needs, based on assessments, which can be observational, via portfolios, rubrics, or projects.

Source: https://michiganvirtual.org/research/publications/student-centered-learning-in-principle-and-in-practice/

Child Gifted Program

We will develop a premium child gifted program for advanced preschoolers. We will choose students based on specialty test scores, full assessments, and teacher observations regarding:

1.   Excellent Memory
2.   Knowledge Retention
3.   Language Skills
4.   Speaking and Talking Fluency
5.   Gross and Fine Motor Skills

Resources: www.davidsongifted.org/prospective-families/is-my-child-gifted/
             www.davidsongifted.org/gifted-blog/frequently-asked-questions-about-extreme-intelligence-in-very-young-children/
Source: https://rainforestlearningcentre.ca/is-my-toddler-or-preschooler-gifted-what-are-the-early-signs-of-intellectual-giftedness/

National Association for Gifted Children   https://nagc.org/
NAGC is the nation's leading organization focused on the needs of gifted and talented children.

Private Pre-K and Kindergarten Programs

We will develop advanced and personalized Pre-K and Kindergarten curriculum-based programs that will prepare students to excel in the latter grades. This will primarily result from the small class size, low child-to-adult ratios, specially-designed and accredited curriculum, continuous dialogue and feedback loop with the parents, milestone accomplishment celebrations, and the opportunity for dedicated attention from a qualified, degreed teacher.

There will also be a focus on the development of the following essential skills:
1.   Independent reading
2.   Creative writing to communicate ideas
3.   Math knowledge, including problem solving and measuring.
4.   Mastering the scientific method to study the environment.
5.   Phonemic awareness and literacy comprehension.
6.   Activities that focus on social skills development.

Example: www.childtime.com/educational-programs/curriculum/private-kindergarten/
         www.cadence-education.com/programs/private-kindergarten/

Personalized Instruction Service

We will offer this service to parents that want their child to have more one-on-one teacher interactions and support, for extra or advanced learning purposes. These parents will have the financial means to basically provide their child with personalized, private tutoring services, as opposed to the usual group-based programs.

Example: www.edelements.com/services/personalized-learning-instruction
Resource: https://personalizedlearningforall.com/

Personalized Toddler Program

We will develop a personalized curriculum after observing and assessing the child's developmental progress with questionnaires and trained screeners and observers. We will create the student's schedule, in real-time, based on weekly updates about academic progress and interest developments. Our objective will be to provide these families with the right insights and best-fit tips to help support their child on the learning journey and to make the right program choices.

The Personalized Toddler Program will use the following advanced education philosophies:
1.   Strengthening bilingual language skills
2.   Refining gross and fine motor skills with modified sports activities
3.   Developing independence and self-confidence via a constructive feedback loop
4.   Practicing social skills in small and large group settings
5.   Learning about empathy to care for others
6.   Increasing frequency of insightful progress reports sent to parents with provisions for more comments to increase dialoguing opportunities.
7.   Programing to include recommended at-home support systems and room designs.
8.   Accessing more educational toys and games.
9.   Developing critical thinking problem solving skills.
10.   Tracking of child progress against development milestones.
Source: https://parentpowered.com/personalized-learning/

Dual Language Education Program

The dual language program will be an additive bilingual program, because all students will develop and maintain their home language, while adding a second language to their repertoire. This program will offer fluency in two languages, (English and Spanish?), which research indicates is best accomplished at an early age. Being bilingual will help these children to maintain strong ties with their family, culture, and community.

Examples: https://adventschoolboca.org/dual-language-prek/
              https://www.arborland.com/dual-language

XII.   Part-time Care Services

The growing need for part-time care services has resulted from the following factors:
1.   A growing gig economy that needs more freelance works.
2.   The increasing expense of full-time childcare.
3.   Difficulty of finding and scheduling qualified and prescreened babysitters.

We will offer part-time care as a means to maximize the utilization of the facility's capacity, improve the profit margins, increase the facilities' visibility, and make part-time flexibility into a competitive advantage. To make our facility competitive, we will get our business accredited, hire friendly and energetic caregivers, segment children based on age groups, and offer a diverse range of programs.

We will use the following tactics to make part-time care profitable:
1.   Charge a 20% premium on part-time spots: divide the full-time rate by the number of hours committed to in that rate and then add a 20% premium to that hourly rate.
2.   Actively look for part-time students that have complementary schedules, such as one in the morning, and one in the afternoon.
3.   Use part-timers to fill gaps or holes in the schedule to increase profitability.

Directory: www.care.com/part-time-daycare
Examples: www.wonderschool.com/p/parent-resources/part-time-daycare/
              https://austinchildrensacademy.org/part-time-care-program/

Flexible Drop-in Daycare Program
We will establish a Flex Drop-in Daycare Program whereby parents can purchase child care days in advance, to be used as needed, throughout the year. This program will help the preschool to better plan for the necessary resources to handle this sporadic type of business, and benefit from the predictable cashflow from the prepaid cards. The drop-in daycare program will also increase the visibility of the preschool and expose more children to our summer camp program.

This Flex Daycare Program will be the perfect solution for parents with the following needs:
1.   Need daycare services over closed school holidays and/or spring breaks.
2.   Work part-time or have an irregular work or volunteer schedule.
3.   Work or stay-at-home, but need an occasional sanity "day off".
4.   Need childcare to handle beauty appointments or medical emergencies.
5.   Want their child enrolled only a couple of weeks in the summer program.
6.   Want their homeschooled child to occasionally have other learning and social interaction experiences.

Parents will be able to purchase prepaid flex daycare cards, in five-day bundles, through our preschool website or front desk. Each card will be valid for one full year. There will be no limit as to how many days the card can be purchased for, in advance. As an added bonus, there will be no extra fees, at either the time of purchase, or when the daycare service is actually used. After completing the enrollment paperwork and submitting payment, parents will be able to call __ (24?) hours in advance to reserve their daycare appointment. Parents will be regularly given satisfaction surveys and the opportunity to benefit from the referral program.

Example: https://www.lapetite.com/educational-programs/drop-in-care/

Summer Camps

Our summer camp will allow students to continue fun-filled learning throughout the summer months, and/or get a head start on the coming new school year. The children will benefit from outdoor playtime and physical activity and healthy, delicious meals and snacks, which will enable them to stay active throughout the day. Field trips will be offered to enable our campers to explore the community, while in-school visitors and events will be designed to deliver new experiences.

Examples: www.lapetite.com/educational-programs/summer-camp/
                www.thegardnerschool.com/camp-gardner/
                https://kiddingaroundcolumbia.com/guide_categories/preschool-summer-camps-columbia

Vacation Care Programs

Our vacation care programs will be designed to include a variety of experiences, ranging from excursions into the community as well as field trips. We will offer a variety of physical activities, project work and lessons. We will develop an engaging weekly program, with various themes, for each school holiday period. We will promote this program as an opportunity for children to make new friends, experience new activities, and socialize with other children of different ages and diverse backgrounds.

Example: http://www.goodstart.org.au/vacation-care

Mini-Camps

We offer mini-camps throughout the school year, usually for one-week spans, when some schools close for holiday recess periods, and working parents need to make other childcare arrangements. We will offer half day, full day and extended day mini-camp options.

Examples: https://www.esfcamps.com/camps-experiences/mini/
                https://www.greenville.explorerkids.us/preschool-summer-mini-camp
                https://www.esfcamps.com/chestnuthill/programs/mini-camp/

XIII. Develop Related Business Subsidiaries

Mobile Birthday Party Bus
The bus will handle up to ___ (16?) children at a time, ages 18mo-7yrs. We will offer the option of one, two- or three-hour packages. Other package options will include child goodie bags, balloon art, DJ, photographer, birthday cake, and healthy snacks and beverages. The bus will have pre-hung party decorations, and children will be able to tumble on mattresses, and play games, such as ring toss, magnetic darts, basketball hoop shooting, heavy bag punching, rock wall climbing, cornhole, and perform songs and dances, set to their favorite pre-arranged music playlist. There will also be a craft making and art painting sessions, supervised by art instructors, and a portable bicycle riding obstacle course. We will circulate flyers, with discount coupons, to all enrolled families, and ask parents to post their positives reviews on social media accounts and our website. Customers will have the option to have the party either conducted on the bus and surrounding area, or have the contracted party rental equipped setup in the home or backyard, on soft play mattresses.

Examples: https://funbuses.com/south-palm-beach/parties-events/birthday-parties
               www.facebook.com/people/Fun-Bus-South-Palm-Beach-Broward-County/100046372673543/?ref=br_rs
               https://tinybeans.com/socal/the-most-convenient-birthday-parties-ever/
               https://artbarnkids.com/pages/special-events-birthday-parties

Mobile Children's Fitness Gym Bus
We will build a mobile gym on wheels and offer 45-minute fitness classes to daycares, childcare centers, rec centers, preschools, church days, and other childcare facilities, with children ages 18 months to 7yrs, on a weekly rotating schedule. It will be a mobile, fun and safe environment. This mobile bus business will specialize in the servicing of summer camps, school events, religious events, corporate events and birthday parties. The onboard coaches will help children to build muscles and healthy habits, and families to build memories. The program focus will be on developing upper body strength, lower body strength, balance, coordination, and fine-and gross-motor skills. Our classes will include gymnastics, cheer, dance, shadow boxing, ninja, tumbling, and fitness. They will all come with a comprehensive curriculum that allows children to grow in many areas. Parents will be able to use our app to ask questions, register online and access the video surveillance feed, during the program. We will assign two professionally trained fitness instructors to each bus. They will lead children through skills and drills, courses and games on kid approved gym equipment, which will be assembled both inside and outside the bus. We will also offer portable obstacle courses, climbing walls, tumbling mattresses, and bounce houses.

Examples: https://funbuses.com/south-palm-beach
               https://www.gymskills.com/mobile-gym
Franchise   https://mygymfranchise.com/franchise-models-costs/mobile/

Tutoring Services
We plan to offer tutoring services for preschool, and elementary school students. We will

help children who need the one-on-one attention of a tutor to help them make literacy discoveries such as: reading aloud, understanding key concepts, recalling story parts, and how-to make reading books fun and interesting. Our primary objective will be to provide the educational foundations that will enable preschoolers to excel and perhaps, even skip early grades, when they get to the elementary or grammar school. We will make the tutoring sessions more fun by incorporating games, singing action songs, getting to know the student needs, and enabling more interactivity. Tutoring will be for 45 minutes, and a tutor will be matched in a 1:1 relationship with a student. We will also supplement tutoring sessions with online learning programs.

Tutoring subjects will include:

Reading	Math
Writing	Spelling
Critical Thinking	Homeschool Support
Early Reading	Reading Comprehension

Examples: https://www.whizkidstutoring.com/elementary
                      https://alacartelearning.com/reading/
Resources: www.readingrockets.org/topics/afterschool-and-community-
                      programs/articles/tutoring-strategies-preschool-and-kindergarten

Mobile Tutoring Services

Our goal will be to deliver hyper-personalized, on-demand, and tech-enabled tutoring services to early childhood learning students. We will also offer package deals that ensure that the tutoring sessions happen regularly with the same tutor over a period of time. We will also differentiate our program by developing the tools to start the program by assessing student learning gaps, and then delivering personalized instruction. We will also help qualified families to locate public funding programs. We will help them to apply for state scholarships, high-dosage tutoring financial assistance, and/or government-funded grants.

FL Examples:
www.fldoe.org/schools/school-choice/k-12-scholarship-programs/reading/
www.fldoe.org/schools/school-choice/k-12-scholarship-programs/fes/
https://www.stepupforstudents.org/

We will use the following marketing tactics to grow our tutoring services business:
1.   Circulate discount coupons for first trial lesson.
2.   Offer a free consultation call or session.
3.   Post flyers on bulletin boards in libraries, grocery stores, recreational centers, etc.
4.   Participate in parenting forums and Facebook Groups.
        Resources: www.facebook.com/groups/category/parenting/
                            www.facebook.com/groups/parentingcommunitygroup/
                            www.facebook.com/groups/409023036225231/
                            https://forums.feedspot.com/parenting_forums/
        Example: www.mumsnet.com/talk/parenting
5.   Establish mutual referral and networking relationships with local daycares,

other preschools, and public and charter schools.
6.   Build website with tutor resumes, scheduling functionality, tutoring blog, unique value proposition statements, positive testimonials, frequently asked questions, and an online demo lesson.
7.   Circulate business cards with logo, multiple contact options and certifications.
8.   Build database to launch direct email advertising program.
        Resource: www.constantcontact.com/blog/how-to-advertise-tutoring/
9.   Establish referral program with real incentives.
10.   Get listed on an online tutoring services directory.
        Directory: https://www.privatetutordirectory.com/
                        https://www.tutorindex.com/
                        https://studentsupportaccelerator.org/database/tutoring
Resource: https://tutorcruncher.com/tutoring-online/where-to-advertise-tutoring-services/

Develop a pricing strategy based on the following factors:
1.   The time cost and expense of travel to the student's home or library.
2.   The value of the service and lesson plans being offered.
3.   The Certifications earned by the tutor.
4.   The branded reputation of the tutoring service.
5.   The assembling of a multi-session tutoring package.

Develop a lesson plan based on the following steps:
1.   Build rapport with the student by asking about their school experiences or interests.
2.   Review the concept introduced at the last session.
3.   Describe the goals for the new session.
4.   Introduce the tutoring materials and templates for the session.
5.   Teach the new concept.
6.   Practice the new concept using tutoring materials.
7.   Review related schoolwork.
8.   Play a fun learning game using the new concept.
9.   Summarize the key takeaways from the session.
10.   Create a short homework assignment to be used to practice the lesson.
11.   Leave time to answer student questions.
12.   Make assessment notes, as to student progress, on the student assigned webpage.
13.   Make arrangements for the next session.
14.   Post the password-protected lesson plan to the company website for future reference by the student and/or family.

Examples: https://www.gradepotentialtutoring.com/
              https://www.khanacademy.org/
              https://huntingtonhelps.com/

Mobile Classroom and Bookmobile
We will build a combination mobile classroom and bookstore, in a reconditioned school bus, and use it for community outreach purposes. We will go out into the community and give

sample goodwill demonstration lessons to children and their parents. We will also use the bus to facilitate class trips and use side panel signage, as a moveable billboard, to promote brand awareness and the location of our preschool. We will also use the truck to pick-up and drop-off after-school enrichment program students, whose families agree to pay an added fee for this transportation service. The truck may also play a role in servicing our mobile birthday party business, and the selling of books at fairs and festivals. A portion of our stock will come from customers who want to trade their books for store credit. We will also handle used children's books on a consignment basis. We will make certain to comply with the local by-laws governing street retail and research the cost of selling at mobile vending events. We will also publish rental rates for private events, such as $500 for a two-hour event, which will include $250 in books.

Vehicle Source: www.msvehicles.com/specialty-vehicles/bookmobiles
Examples: https://irondogbooks.com/book-trade-in-program
            https://www.riverbendbookshop.com/BookTruck
Resource: https://bookriot.com/how-to-start-a-bookmobile/
Association of Bookmobile and Outreach Services   https://abos-outreach.com/

Babysitting Services

We plan to offer a baby sitter referral service, and collect a referral service fee. Our preschool management team will screen and train babysitters with our own in-house developed manuals, videos and training programs, and then charge them an initial fee to be listed in our directory. Parents needing babysitting would then pay an initial registration fee to be able to call in for recommendations on sitters, and we would collect a percent of the babysitter fee.

Resources: https://safesitter.org/caring-for-preschoolers/
            https://kidsit.com/how-to-babysit-preschoolers
Job Board   https://upwards.com/jobs

On-Demand Babysitter

We will build an app that matches families to extensively pre-screened caregivers, provides meeting scheduling, continuous monitoring access and processes the final secure payment.

Examples: https://www.weesitt.com/#vettedsitters
            https://www.bambinositters.com/

Montessori Nanny Training Academy

We will train these nannies how to create a nurturing and stimulating environment that supports children's natural development. The certification process will involve gaining childcare experience, earning a degree associated with Montessori, creating a nanny profile, and getting CPR and first-aid certification.

Resources: https://montessoritoddler.com/blog/how-to-be-a-montessori-nanny/
            https://amshq.org/Educators/Montessori-Careers/Become-a-Montessori-Educator/About-AMS-TEP/Find-A-TEP

Nanny and Babysitter Placement Agency Services

We will connect families with experienced nannies and babysitters, who will provide developmental child care with ____ (Montessori?) early childhood education philosophies. This placement staffing agency will be a subsidiary of our preschool business. Whether the client looking to cover the occasional date night or require more consistent care for their children, we will provide the comprehensive solution.

Examples: https://nannies.wildroots.com

Virtual Babysitting/Nanny Services

Our virtual babysitters will entertain children and keep them engaged, with appropriate activities, via video calls, when in-person babysitting isn't an option. This service will help families to maintain the household chores, assist with homeschooling and entertain their children while working from home. We will keep children actively engaged in small group "virtual babysitting" sessions, filled with fun, social, and creative activities. We will use the following platforms: Zoom, Google Hangout, FaceTime and WhatsApp. Sessions will revolve around the following activities: storytelling, singing, dancing, reading aloud, pretend play, crafting and number counting.

Example: https://virtualbabysittersclub.com
Resource: https://3veta.com/blog/business-advice/virtual-babysitting-and-how-to-
               become-a-virtual-nanny/
               https://blog.urbansitter.com/what-is-a-virtual-babysitter/

After School Care

We will conduct surveys and interviews to determine the needs of parents and offer convenient hours that fit with their parenting and work schedules. Most afterschool programs operate during the hours after school, usually from around 3:00 PM to 6:00 PM, and offer extracurricular activities to help children learn new skills, such as technology, art and dance.

Resource: https://www.care.com/c/unique-after-school-programs/
               https://www.care.com/c/10-options-for-after-school-child-care/
Directory:
www.merakilane.com/what-to-do-after-school-31-after-school-activities-for-kids/

Second Shift Care

This program will be appropriate in manufacturing towns that have multiple work shifts. Other targeted groups will be: hospital employees, hotel, bar and restaurant staffers, police officers, and retail workers. We will offer 24-hour scheduling options. which will include early morning, evening, or late-night childcare. We will work with employers to create a child care center that offers customized services for combined company employees.

Resources: https://www.fcrnew.org/blog/2nd-shift-and-childcare/
https://winnie.com/resources/finding-childcare-when-you-dont-work-9-to-5
https://info.childcareaware.org/blog/finding-child-care-non-traditional-work-schedules

Expanded/Extended Care Days
We will offer extended hours on days when schools are closed for parent/teacher conferences or curriculum planning days, or during holidays. This will attract families who are looking for child care on days when other preschools or daycare centers are closed.
Example: https://www.albrookschool.org/programs/extended-care/

Weekend Care Services
We plan to expand our childcare and preschool hours of operation to include weekends. As more parents work non-traditional schedules, there is a growing need for childcare hours outside of the 9-5 work day. We will provide meals and snacks, and diapers, which will benefit busy weekend working parents.

Resource: https://winnie.com/resources/what-is-weekend-childcare
Membership Club Example: https://kidsklubcdc.com/evening-weekend/
A Kids Klub membership is required for every child to attend the Evening and Weekend after hours daycare program. 24 hours in advance is appreciated for every child who is planning to attend the program. However, we do accommodate same day reservations and member walk-ins if space permits.

Overnight Care
This service will allow parents to get a night out.
Example: https://firststudentinc.com/our-services/full-service/early-childhood-services/
             https://www.hopskipdrive.com/counties

Special Needs Services
We plan to offer specialized programs, such as programs for children with autism. We will explain our teaching and therapeutic philosophy, and make sure it aligns with the parent's preferences, and serves their child's needs. We will also provide consulting services to parents who want to homeschool their children. To be successful in delivering these programs, we will maintain consistent routines, make children's interests a part of the learning process, provide consistent, positive feedback, and allocate plenty of time for the practicing of new skills.
Resources: www.verywellhealth.com/preschool-and-autism-whats-the-best-choice-260140
Source: https://mybrightwheel.com/blog/teaching-preschoolers-with-autism

XIV. Teacher Training and Staffing Agency

Preschool Teacher Training Academy
We will develop an online Teacher Training and Resource Center that includes a database of more than _____ (10,000?) custom lesson plans, based on progressive new teaching methods. The center will help teachers learn their craft, customize lesson plans based on student's needs and capabilities, improve their organizational, communication and interpersonal skills, and give them a chance to connect across the preschool teacher's network.

Examples:	www.udemy.com/course/how-to-teach-any-subject-to-young-children/
	www.montessoritrainingusa.com/
Resources:	https://amshq.org/Educators/Montessori-Careers/Become-a-Montessori-Educator
	www.cceionline.com/professional-development-courses-teacher/
	https://www.naeyc.org/resources/topics/training
Source:	https://www.preschoolteacher.org
Online:	https://www.montessoritraining.net/

Google for Education
https://edu.google.com/for-educators/training-courses/?modal_active=none
https://edu.google.com/intl/ALL_us/for-educators/training-courses/?modal_active=none

Preschool Assistant Teacher Training Program

We will provide the mentoring support to start a job as a preschool assistant teacher or work with children at a daycare. We will guide attendees as to what free certificates and online training are available to build a resume and portfolio, and how-to have a successful job interview. We will share the links for classes and all the required certificates and training to start working at a preschool or a day care. We will also provide free training at our preschool to realize assistant teacher status.

Example:	www.eventbrite.com/e/preschool-teacher-training-tickets-895624104807
	https://learn.org/articles/requirements_to_become_a_preschool_teacher_
	assistant_in_california.html

Preschool Teacher and Admin Staffing Agency
We will use our staffing agency to place fully trained and vetted teachers, assistants and directors to child care centers, preschools and afterschool programs. Our vetting process will start with mandatory and comprehensive background screening, and will include behavioral and structural interviews with all job candidates. Substitute teachers will also be available on-demand, for same day, short-term assignments, long-term assignments or permanent placements. Our recruiters will be fully trained on being compliant all state licensing requirements. We will also help our recruited teachers to maintain a healthy work/life balance in their careers. We will help our clients to have the flexibility to easily maintain the state required child-to-staff ratios. Our training programs will directly feed qualified candidates to our staffing agency. Our target markers will be public schools, private schools and childcare centers with preschool programs.

Examples: https://www.childcarecareers.com/
https://the-piazza.net/join-piazza/preschool-substitute-teacher/
www.kellyeducation.com/services-and-solutions/recruiting-and-hiring/
screening-and-accreditation
https://www.tempositions.com/preschool-teacher/

XV.   Engagement and Retention Strategies

Foster Family Engagement

In our preschool, family engagement will be a collaborative and strengths-based process, through which early childhood professionals, families, and children will build positive and goal-oriented relationships. We will foster family engagement by opening the lines of communication between home and preschool, which will be the key to building a feedback-loop, that will enrich the child's experience at the preschool.

We will host public-welcome events at our school to achieve the following objectives:
1. Develop deeper relationships with parent customers.
2. Establish a reputation for sharing our child development expertise.
3. Increase the preschool visibility by welcoming prospective families and the friends of families.
4. Generate new revenue streams by offering fee-based advanced seminars and personalized coaching services on hot trending topics.

Build a Sense of Community

We will host family events so that parents, not only feel connected to the preschool, but also to each other. Typical types of family-inspired events will include:
1. Organize Mother's and Father's Day Breakfasts
2. Plan field trips to local waterpark, museum, zoo or aquarium.
3. Schedule a day at the movies
4. Hold a picnic or barbeque in a city park.
5. Stage a pizza party at a recreational center
6. Arrange 'Mommy and Me' Yoga Sessions
7. Conduct workshops on parenting and child social development.
8. Hold child art exhibitions at the library and community center.
9. Plant a community vegetable garden.
10. Host buddy days with older children.
11. Conduct visits to local fire halls, police stations and/or first responder ambulance companies.
12. Greet parents in the morning and afternoon at the front of the building, so parents can see the faces of those responsible for the well-being of their children.

Foster Community Engagement

We will service the needs of the local community to build the goodwill of the business. We will take the following actions to support the local community:
1. Source supplies locally.
2. Recruit teachers from the community.
3. Support community activities with donations, such as fundraisers, education programs, school sporting events, cleanup drives, food, toy and clothing drives, recycling and composting projects, and main street parades.
4. Provide volunteer work at nursing homes, animal shelters and soup kitchens.
5. Hold workshops that help parents to solve their child raising challenges.
6. Stay in tune with the changing needs of parents, and think in terms of providing multi-dimensional, life-centric support.

Resource: https://rainforestlearningcentre.ca/community-service-learning-ideas-for-early-childhood-education-and-daycare/

Support the Business Community
We will build long-term relationships with local businesses by sponsoring some of their promotional events. Our objective will be to create mutual referral relationships and to benefit from joint publicity campaigns. We will show our support for the business community by sourcing our products and services from local businesses, giving them an information presentation platform at our preschool, and distributing alliance partner discount coupons.

Form Partnerships with Local Businesses
We will form cross-promotion, mutual referral relationships, with the following types of local businesses:

1.	Hospitals	Distribute new born gift baskets with logo-imprinted toys, Labeled children's books and discount tuition coupons.
2.	Churches	Establish space sharing or room sub-leasing relationships
3.	Bookstore	Host story-time sessions
4.	Craft Store	Host arts and crafts sessions
5.	Cafes	Display upcoming enrollment flyers
6.	Baby Boutiques	Place summer camp postcards in counter displays
7.	Kid Barber Shops	Distribute free consultation and tour coupons
8.	Toy Stores	Conduct workshops on the benefits of educational toys.
9.	Ice Cream Shops	Distribute free tickets to a coming event.
10.	Pediatricians	Giveaway educational toys with log-imprinted labels.
11.	Supermarkets	Post flyers on their bulletin board.
12.	Libraries	Host story-time sessions.

Setup Parent Advisory Council (PAC)
The goal of the parent advisory council will be to help the preschool to attain its goal of providing each child with the best education and social development experiences, and guiding the school toward continuous improvement. We will setup a Parent Advisory Council that will consist of 4 to 6 parents, two teachers, community outreach officer, School Director, and the Head-of-School. The parents and teachers will be on a rotating one-year membership cycle. We will also welcome guests from the community and

expert speakers on early child development.

The PAC will meet monthly or four times per year, and perform the following functions:
1. Assist in the strategic planning process via collaborative brainstorming sessions.
2. Give parents a place to vent their problems with the preschool and obtain solutions.
3. Be a forum that gives parents a voice and a means to share ideas and best practices.
4. Build community support by facilitating the flow of resident insights and business sponsorships.
5. Make marketing campaign suggestions and facilitate the making of networking connections.
6. Coordinate the holding of fundraisers throughout the year.
7. Assignment of projects to volunteer workgroups.
8. Become the liaison between families and the preschool.
9. Investigate the opportunity to secure grants for school projects.

We will promote the Parent Advisory Council (PAC) in the following ways:
1. Create a Facebook Group to increase awareness and communications.
2. Post meeting minutes to the preschool newsletter and website page.
3. Post videos of council member interviews and council meetings to YouTube.
4. Use rewards and incentives to motivate our PAC to drive more family referrals.

Examples: www.pacoimacharterpreschool.com/parent-advisory-council
             https://earlychildhood.rdale.org/discover/parent-advisory-committeel-pac
             https://www.ovsd.org/domain/851

Source: www.solvedconsulting.com/blog/your-simple-guide-to-creating-a-parent-advisory-committee-pac

Establish Community Outreach Program

We will develop a community outreach program, with assigned staffers, that serve the following functions:
1. Works with local businesses to develop mutual referral programs and solicit sponsors for school fundraisers.
2. Circulates questionnaires that help parents to determine what level and type of early developmental support is needed for their child.
3. Conducts assessments of children using direct observation and interaction protocols to determine child early education and social development needs.
4. Consults with clinicians to discuss a range of health monitoring recommendations and develop action plans.
5. Organizes workshops for daycares and other community agencies to educate about different child development specialties.
6. Advises community members and partners on the benefits of transitioning out of daycare into early education preschool to be ready for higher school grades.
7. Partners with local libraries, parks, planetariums, botanical gardens and children's museums to provide more opportunities for the mutual referral of early

child development programs.
8. Supports caregivers/families by providing access to our support services and resources.
9. Reviews enrollment data to spot trends and improve outreach operations.
10. Reaches out to children from underserved communities, with tuition funding options, so they can benefit from the advantages of early education.
11. Conducts classroom observations, parent support meetings, and home visits as needed, to establish and maintain productive relationships with preschool families.
12. Offers literacy workshops and parenting classes to demonstrate a commitment to community welfare.

Resource: https://www.naeyc.org/resources/topics/community-outreach
https://www.newamerica.org/new-practice-lab/briefs/family-outreach-for-early-education-enrollment/

Example: https://www.opendoorpreschool.org/jobs-program-specialist
https://westminster-co.geebo.com/jobs-online/view/id/1370379202-universal-preschool-outreach-specialist-/

Host Parenting Workshops and Seminars

We plan to offer a series of ongoing or one-shot parenting workshops and seminars that will be offered to parents to provide practical advice on a wide range of problems they encounter in raising children. Topics will include:

First aid remedies for children
Dealing with aggression
Developing a positive self-image
Fostering a sense of independence
Dealing with attention deficit disorder
Handling discipline and behavior problems
Addressing sleep issues
Discussing sex issues
Mastering potty training
Nutrition guidelines for children
Exercise programs for children
Talking with children
Designing children's rooms to stimulate creativity.

Train Parents to Raise Child Contributors

We will develop a parent training program that not only teaches parents how-to coach their children on how to be more independent, but also who want to contribute their services to family projects, and resist the natural tendency to become more self-centered and self-absorbed.

We will incorporate the following principles into the program:
1. Give children specific chores to accomplish and praise them for their contributions.

2. Give children the chance to solve problems on their own, and praise them for trying.
3. Let the child make choices, from a set of defined options or parameters, and ask them to explain how they made that choice.
4. Structure the child's day so they can anticipate the role they will play.
5. Start with the assigning of small, simple tasks, and gradually build in more complexity.
6. Tell children how much it is appreciated when they volunteer to help with a project.

Host Family Carnivals

We will host the following types of family carnivals, as combination customer appreciation events and bring-a-friend, open house, marketing events:

Halloween Parties	Easter Egg Hunts
Arts and Crafts Fairs	Music Festivals
Bicycle Tours	Runners Marathons
Musical Entertainment	Magician Shows
Bounce House Events	Obstacle Course Competitions
Kite Flying Contests	

Host Local Event Booths

We will setup exhibition display booths at the following types of events to circulate our marketing materials, and award door prizes, such as educational playsets and coloring books, and healthy snacks and beverages, with our logo imprinted labels:

Park Easter Egg Hunts	Music Festivals
Family Fun Festivals	Chamber of Commerce Events
Holiday Bazaars	Swap Meets
Health Checkups	Child Assessments

Rent Temporary Pop-Up Retail Spaces

During prime retailing seasons, we will rent temporary pop-up storefronts to accomplish the following marketing and sales objectives at low startup costs:
1. Meet with parents to schedule preschool tours.
2. Offer early preschool registration discounts.
3. Distribute our preschool marketing materials.
4. Market children' books, and educational videos, toys and games.
5. Offer children's book authors a chance to present to their targeted audiences.
6. Promote our adult teaching and training academies.

Source:	https://squareup.com/us/en/the-bottom-line/starting-your-business/how-to-open-a-pop-up-shop
Resources:	www.thestorefront.com/ www.peerspace.com/venues/
	www.popshop.com www.popable.com
	https://giggster.com/find/ www.splacer.co/rent/space/

XVI.　　Create Multi-Function Preschool Rooms

Preschool Library and Product Retailing Room
We will expand the preschool reading corner into a room to serve as both the school library and to retail educational toy sets and children's books, that further child development. We will create a room for reading that is separate from the learning rooms. We will feature books and toys that are popular with the students, and have been demonstrated to assist with child development. We will choose products that support both guided and free play, and are durable, eco-friendly, have positive online customer reviews and encourage learning. The various preschool classes will take turns using the library room for one- hour periods. Parents who shop the secure library/retailing room, will need to be cleared by the front desk, except on weekends. We will provide information on the bestsellers and feature parent reviews. We will also make reading recommendations based on child ages, reading level and interests.

We will create a secure direct entrance into this library/sales room, so that parents can shop at anytime without entering the preschool lobby or disturbing the students. We will also treat this area as a reading room or library for the students. To help drive product sales we will write and self-publish articles and books, about the psychological benefits of reading, play and movement for children.

Resource:　　Kindle Direct Publishing

Library/Reading/Retailing: Multi-Purpose Room Design Elements
1. Make it a cozy space, that is, well-lit and sound-proofed, and big enough for a group of children.
2. Create child's reading nook areas, with bean bag chairs, and child sized tables and chairs.
3. Install a colorful rug and comfortable, group child seating, in a half-round arrangement.
4. Provide pillows, that are mobile and adjustable, so students can listen and read how they are most comfortable.
5. Include lots of soft materials and plants, to make the space warm and inviting.
6. Paint with pastel/light/neutral colors to increase concentration.
7. Install low, open shelves and filled with books, educational toys and games and accessories.
8. Organize books by age group, and in alphabetical order, and by literary genre, such as real life stories, fables, poetry, and illustrated books, with a shelf-label system.
9. Provide space to organize reading-related activities, such as storytelling, puppet shows and dramatizations.
10. Install a check-out and customer service counter or desk at the separate exterior entrance to the room.

Examples:　　www.forbes.com/sites/forbes-personal-shopper/article/best-toys-for-4-year-old-boys/?sh=5520a97d7858

Resource:　　www.aap.org/en/practice-management/bright-futures/bright-futures-family-centered-care/well-child-visits-parent-and-patient-education/bright-futures-information-for-parents-4-year-visit/

Source:　　https://blog.kinedu.com/reading-corner/

XVII.   Online Sales Platform

Ecommerce Product Sales
We will customize a standard ecommerce website to sell our logo-imprinted T-shirts, supplies, Books, curriculum kits, and educational toys. Featured products will include Leap Frog computers, sticker books, travel kits, new and used children's books, and video games, Montessori toys, coloring books, water bottles, journals, and properly sized backpacks, diaper bags, tote bags, and lunch boxes.

Software Resource: www.shopify.com
Source: www.forbes.com/sites/forbes-personal-shopper/article/best-backpacks-for-kids/?sh=4bcd63dd7bdb
www.forbes.com/sites/judykoutsky/2020/03/23/6-great-travel-games-for-preschoolers/?sh=1520b545195c

Educational Toy, Game and Book Subscription Plans
Subscribers to this program will enter the child's birth date and interests to get the personalized 'Subscription Play Box' that supports their developmental stage and interests. Customers will be able to choose boxes for specific interests, such as music, mazes, holiday crafts, art, cooking, and robots. Customers will be able to 'subscribe and save' to receive a new box every (?) months or purchase just one box, of toys that stimulate creativity and imagination. Each play box will come with a play guide to ensure the guiding of the child's growth and development. The booklet will explain how to deliver hours of meaningful playtime, and support the child with the development of new skills. These toys will be made of durable, earth-friendly materials, which will make it easy for toys to find a new home, through our recycling and donation programs. Customers will also be able to purchase these toys as gift items or without signing up for the subscription service, via our online catalog. Customers will be able to browse by category, best sellers, price range, age group, new arrivals and gifts. We will also feature customer unboxing videos on our YouTube channel.
Examples: www.meetlalo.com/pages/the-play-boxes
www.cratejoy.com/collections/educational-subscription-boxes
https://lovevery.com/products/the-play-kits
https://www.wired.com/gallery/best-subscription-boxes-for-kids/
https://www.amazon.com/stem-collectibles-books-educational-kids-toys-subscription-boxes/
https://midcities.kidsoutandabout.com/content/23-subscription-boxes-playing-and-learning
Directory: www.usnews.com/360-reviews/family/best-baby-toy-subscriptions

Sales of Preschool Digital Products
Digital products are intangible goods that exist in a digital format. These include e-books, music, digital art, templates, software, digital art, online courses, interactive printables, resource directories, and video games. They will be delivered to customers via online download or email, and will offer the opportunity to provide value and generate passive income, without physical inventory. We will also circulate our early childhood learning and social development skills, and parenting knowledge, by the writing, publishing and producing of e-courses, e-books, e-newsletters, e-workbooks, video tutorials, and podcasts.

Resources: https://help.shopify.com/en/manual/products/digital-service-
              product/digital-downloads
              www.helprange.com/post/selling-pdfs/how-to-sell-your-pdfs-on-shopify
Source: https://blog.mindgrub.com/designing-digital-products-for-kids
              https://www.mailerlite.com/blog/digital-products
Side Hustle: https://thinktankteacher.com/how-and-why-to-start-a-side-hustle-selling-
              digital-products-and-printables-for-kids/

We will also establish a separate website to sell the following items as digital downloads:
1.   Blended Lesson Plans
2.   Activity Kits
3.   Parenting Guidebooks
4.   Preschool Business Plans
5.   Preschool Marketing Plans
6.   Automated Marketing Software Tools
7.   Preschool Management Software
8.   Customizable Family Handbook
Directory: https://checkoutpage.co/blog/18-best-websites-to-sell-digital-products

Distribution of Preschool Product Essentials

We will become a distributor of products that are in-demand by preschools, daycares and homeschoolers. We will either rent warehousing space for these products, such as furniture, outdoor play equipment, storage organizers, educational toys and games, workbooks and manuals, and school and craft supplies, or develop drop-shipping arrangements with the manufacturers. We will market these products through our family subscription service.
We may also establish an affiliate sales relationship, to earn sales commission, with existing online retailers, such as the Amazon Affiliate Marketing Program (https://affiliate-program.amazon.com/).
Examples: www.kaplanco.com/furniture

Make Drop-shipping Arrangements

When an order is placed, we will send the details and payment to a drop-shipping supplier, who will then deliver the product directly to our customer. We will assess the potential of creating direct ship relationships with educational product manufacturers and distributors.

We will realize the following benefits from these arrangements:
1.   No tie-up of capital in the holding of excess product inventory.
2.   Able to assess the demand for a product before investing in stocking it.
3.   Able to create mutually beneficial alliances with vendors that share the same vision.
4.   Fewer out-of-stock situations because the alliance partners maintain the inventory.
5.   Able to share transaction data so vendors can use this visibility into our business to leverage this knowledge to make better buying and product development decisions.
6.   May be able to negotiate longer payment terms with primary vendors.
7.   Alliance partners are more likely to supply marketing materials that we can utilize.

Resources: https://www.dropship.io/blog/how-to-start-dropshipping
https://www.dropship.io/blog/dropshipping-toys
Directory of Drop-shippers: www.shopify.com/blog/dropshipping-suppliers
https://dropshipping.com/article/dropship-toys/
Example: www.doba.com/category/ArDRVWPRBcvZ/dropshipping-learning-education.html
Arrangement Challenges: www.autods.com/blog/dropshipping-tips-strategies/dropshipping-challenges/
Resource:
https://ecommerce.folio3.com/blog/how-to-sell-other-people-products-on-shopify/

Virtual Preschool Membership Program

The target market for these virtual online programs will be:
1.   Parents who homeschool their preschoolers and want added support.
2.   Families who want convenient, afterschool enrichment programs for their children.
3.   Families who value affordable, on-demand, virtual learning opportunities to augment in school lessons, with complementary programs.

We will also sell curriculum resources, which can either be used as the primary curriculum or augment traditional preschool models. We will develop an application questionnaire to help personalize the program to the needs of each student. Our classes will be taught live over Zoom and be delivered by qualified preschool teachers. We will ship a curriculum box full of all the materials the child needs to participate fully in the classes. The curriculum will be structured so each class offers a variety of hands-on learning experiences. Parents can choose 1-day, 2-day, 3-day, or 5-day a week schedules.

This monthly virtual membership program will include:
1.   Live Classes via Zoom with our certified teachers.
2.   Stories, poems, and lesson about the weekly thematic topic.
3.   Game-based learning, focused on developing fine motor and cognitive skills, such as letter identification, numbers, patterns, memory, and concentration.
4.   Home-based craft project suggestions
5.   Storybook read-alouds.
6.   A workbook and printable worksheets to practice writing, phonetics, literacy, math, language arts, science, arts, and social studies.
7.   Feedback from teachers after uploading the child's completed worksheets.
8.   Monthly student progress reports.
9.   Access to a library of musical performances and video tutorials.
10.   Guidance on age-appropriate activities, using interactive multimedia and hands-on materials.
11.   Assistance with the scheduling of weekly playdates to socialize with friends.

Pricing Strategy:
Virtual Online Preschool will cost $__ (99.99?) per month, or $__ (79.99?) per month, if prepaid for the entire year or $____ (24.99) if paid weekly. All class supplies are included in the tuition costs and will be delivered to the home at no cost. There is one-time $___ (50?)

registration fee that covers the student registration and skills assessment processes, and the cost of materials for the lifetime of enrollment.

Examples: https://playtolearnpreschool.us/ptl-virtual-preschool/
              https://playgardenonline.com/virtual-preschool/

Marketing Strategy:
1. Offer access to a free trial class.
    Note: Includes a list of materials needed to participate, most of which can be found around the home.
    Example: https://parent.growingbrilliant.com/enrollment
2. Produce a YouTube box opening video for the curriculum supplies box.
3. Build a website that covers program descriptions, parent testimonials, pricing, frequently asked questions, blog, social media links, and contact options.

Online Video Streaming Subscription Service
We will sell video subscriptions to the following expanded types of content:
1. Parent Training Programs
2. Infant/Toddler Learning and Development Programs
3. Happy Birthday Party Videos
4. Afterschool Enrichment Programs, such as technology and cooking classes.
5. Sing-along videos.
6. Educational Game Videos

Examples:
https://shop.incredibleyears.com/collections/online-video-streaming-for-parent-training-programs
https://cainclusion.org/camap/california-department-of-education-streaming-video-subscription-service-now-available-free/
https://www.caearlylearningvideos.org/
https://kidslearningtubeshop.com/products/video-membership
https://kidoodle.tv/

eLearning Programs
Our goal will be to provide learning experiences tailored to each child. We will deliver online content and lessons that are aligned with the child's interests and learning requirements, within specific age groups. It will make the entire learning process more personalized, effective and enjoyable. We will build or partner with an educational platform that offers users the tools, information and resources they need to facilitate and manage learning for our preschoolers. The platform will have the following key features:
1. Signup   Registration Process
2. Login   Password Protected
3. User Profiles   Backgrounds/Objectives
4. Dashboard   Track Skills Progress
5. Admin Panel   Add/Edit/Delete Content/Users
6. Payments System   Processing Options
7. Notifications   Reminders/Progress Updates
8. Forum   Used to supply answers to questions

Example: https://www.growingbrilliant.com/preschool_alternative/

Revenues will be driven from the following sources:
1.   Advertising fees from partner businesses
2.   Subscription fees from families
3.   Premium service up-sell fees
4.   Course sales commissions

Directory: www.g2.com/products/skillshare/competitors/alternatives
Example: Khan Academy   www.khanacademy.org
Khan Academy offers practice exercises, instructional videos, and a personalized learning
dashboard that empowers learners to study at their own pace in and outside of the classroom.

Resources:
Rocket Learning   http://www.rocketlearning.org/what-we-do/#Parent-Product
They send byte-sized, audio-visual, and gamified lessons to parents that they can practice with
their children at home using readily available household materials.

Reading Eggs   https://readingeggs.com/
Use children's love of games, songs, golden eggs and other rewards to make them feel proud
of their reading, and really motivated to keep exploring and learning.

Epic Reading   www.getepic.com
A digital reading platform built on a collection of 40,000+ popular, high-quality books from
250+ of the world's best publishers, that fuels curiosity and reading confidence for kids 12 and
under.

Hapara   www.hapara.com
Teachers use Hāpara to see where students are on their learning path. Hāpara tools also help
teachers streamline their workflows, including differentiating digital instruction, personalizing
learning and giving feedback.

Produce Preschooler Educational Videos
We will produce learning videos about ABC songs, toy playing, or bedtime stories. We will
demonstrate our fun and appropriate content based on cartoons, whiteboards, or presentations.
We will produce videos to influence buying behavior, drive more traffic to our site and
encourage more social media shares.

Video Monetization Strategies:
We will use the following strategies to monetize the production of educational videos for
preschoolers:
1.   Join the YouTube Partners Program
        Resource:
        https://blog.youtube/news-and-events/more-ways-for-creators-to-earn-on-youtube/
2.   Offer an Online Course
        Resource: www.learnworlds.com/how-to-sell-online-courses/

Directory: www.learnworlds.com/best-online-course-platforms/
3.   Build Online School or Academy
     Resource: www.learnworlds.com/how-to-start-an-online-school/
4.   Get Brand Sponsorships
     Resource: www.wildapricot.com/blog/how-to-get-sponsorship
5.   Sell Memberships to pre-recorded video courses with premium content
     Resource: www.learnworlds.com/membership-site/
6.   Use Google Adsense to receive payments for advertising on our videos.
     Resource: https://support.google.com/youtube/answer/6162278?hl=en
7.   Sell Branded Merchandise
     Resource: https://printify.com/
8.   Earn commissions from Affiliate Marketing Programs for related products.
     Example: https://affiliate-program.amazon.com/

Source: www.techsmith.com/blog/instructional-videos/
             www.learnworlds.com/how-to-make-tutorial-video-with-examples/
             www.learnworlds.com/video-based-learning/

Directory: Best YouTube Educational Channels
             https://offeo.com/learn/best-educational-youtube-channels
https://kidsinfinitelearning.com/30-best-educational-youtube-channels-for-kids-in-2022/

YouTube Teachers   www.youtube.com/teachers
YouTube.com/Teachers was created to help teachers leverage video to educate, engage
and inspire their students.

Examples:
Toy Kitchen Cooking   www.youtube.com/watch?v=6Pl9x8DkENY
Make Fruit with Play Doh www.youtube.com/watch?v=QyRTnv9ipnw
Art for Kids Hub   www.youtube.com/user/artforkidshub
Preschool Learning Videos www.youtube.com/watch?v=2vYqjQnm3WY

Resources:
Flex Clip   www.flexclip.com/create/preschool-video.html
                         www.flexclip.com/create/education-video.html
This free preschool video maker provides a convenient way to show teaching ideas, like
creating viral videos to upload on YouTube, Facebook, and other platforms. Provides free
preschool video templates, and AI tools for accelerating the editing process, such as AI
text-to-speech, AI text-to-video, etc.

Synthesia   www.synthesia.io/learn/training-videos/educational-video
An AI-powered video maker that comes with AI video presenters that look like real humans
talking in various languages, and includes readymade video templates.

Camtasia   www.techsmith.com/camtasia/
Provides a range of advanced recording and editing tools.

Canva   www.canva.com/features/ai-video-generator/
Use the text-to-video AI generator on Canva to dream up ideas and transform words into stand-out videos that seamlessly fit any project.

We Video   www.wevideo.com
In interactive video learning and editing platform. Gives users the ability to create videos and other types of media to exercise their creativity, work in an authentic, real-world way, and practice their communication and critical thinking skills.

Interactive Kids' Media Analysis

We will install a widescreen TV in the preschool and feature child media episodes that have storytelling and design themes that can have inspirational characters, and a positive impact on child development. We will run segments of these shows and then conduct an interactive analysis of the story in the classroom. Our goal will be to help the students to realize the child development potential of these programs, by holding intermittent group discussions about big picture lessons learned. We will feature kid-oriented shows for preschoolers that may be entertaining enough for older kids. We will ask questions that help to cultivate an understanding of the episode's plot, background concepts, and the essence of the characters. A key focus will be on learning about the importance of tolerance and respect for peoples from different backgrounds.

Examples:
Gabby's Dollhouse   www.dreamworks.com/shows/gabbys-dollhouse
Blues Clues   https://bluesclues.fandom.com/wiki/Blue%27s_Clues_Wiki
Creative Galaxy   https://9story.com/portfolio/creative-galaxy/
Ridley Jones   https://www.netflix.com/title/81074666
Muppet Babies   https://disneynow.com/show/2220df10-86e1-414f-8091-deb2c9b7989d
Marvel's Spidey   https://disneynow.com/show/03f2c0d6-967e-4868-929a-8f2089ce7a85

Source: www.forbes.com/sites/meimeifox/2023/11/21/gabbys-dollhouse-creator-
                      traci-paige-johnson-on-how-to-make-it-in-kids-tv/?sh=5b69750126a4

XVIII.   Growth Without Physical Assets

Collaborate with Local Corporations

We will build or expand our preschool businesses by collaborating with local corporations to determine the following facts:

1. The kinds of shared benefits they want to extend to their employees
2. What scheduling requirements need to be addressed
3. The curriculum they want developed and offered.
4. The management role they want to play.
5. The classroom space and access controls they have available or can assemble.

Preschool collaborations with local businesses will help them to grow by creating value, enhancing education quality, and reducing childcare costs. They will help to design facilities around a known number of to-be enrolled students. It is expected that preschool collaboration will also enhance innovation, increase operational efficiency, open lines of communications, expand the range of services offered, reduce marketing costs, and improve customer satisfaction and loyalty. This type of collaboration will also improve access to both private and public funding sources.

We will also highlight the fact that we will help these businesses to participate in community events that will strengthen community ties, generate goodwill and enhance their brand image. We will collaborate with these preschool founding or supporting businesses on organizing local festivals, sponsoring charity drives, and/or designing educational workshops that will benefit the wider community.

Source:
https://www.childcaremarketing.com/community-partners-for-your-center/
https://fastercapital.com/content/Preschool-Collaboration--Building-
        Successful-Partnerships--Preschool-Collaboration-for-Business-Growth.html
https://childcaredaily.org/building-strong-connections-developing-partnerships-with-local-schools-
        organizations-or-businesses/
Resources:
Bezos Academy   https://bezosacademy.org/
It aims to nurture the potential in every child to become a creative leader, original thinker, and lifelong learner by increasing access to early childhood education in under-resourced communities. It is a network of tuition-free, Montessori-inspired preschools
Bezos Day One Foundation   www.bezosdayonefund.org/day1familiesfund

Preschool as a Business Employee Benefit

We will require the following value return, from the giving of industry discounts to employers, which are typically, in the 10 percent range, to help increase enrollments:

1. Active promotion of our preschool to their employees, such as via the company newsletter.
2. The generation of positive press by the company.
3. The driving of traffic to our preschool or website.
4. The circulation of our marketing materials, with positive employee reviews and testimonials.

5. The opportunity to speak to employees about the motor skills and social development benefits of attending preschool.
Source: https://incentfit.com/wellness-word/day-care-benefits-for-employees-how-to-offer-them/

We will take the following actions so that local mid-sized businesses can offer preschool education, at our location, as part of a 'Preferred Employer Benefits Program':
1. Create a special program for the employees of partnering businesses.
2. Negotiate with these corporations to partially or fully subsidize this employee benefit.
2. Give these customers a special tuition discount or do not charge a registration fee.
3. Assemble a sales presentation portfolio that features the testimonials of the presently enrolled parents, who also work for the targeted businesses.
4. Educate corporations as to the advantages of such an arrangement, including increased productivity, reduced employee absences, greater employee retention and possible tax credits.
5. Help these corporations to publish inserts for their HR hire packets, that explains this real employee benefit, in terms of the potential for a greater work/life balance.
Source: https://www.compt.io/child-care-benefits-for-employees

Employer Childcare Solutions
We will work with local businesses or employers, that want to offer childcare as an on-site benefit to their employees, and create customized daycare solution options for their workforce. We will offer flexible daycare programs for children ages 2 months to 7 years. This will help these companies to attract and retain talent, reduce absenteeism, increase productivity, and receive corporate tax benefits. Reliable on-site preschool and back-up daycare programs will also help to avoid breakdowns in care, reduce commute times, and allow workers to concentrate more fully on their jobs. We will also help these businesses to design and manage conveniently located on-site daycare programs, as a partnership arrangement.
Resource: www.getbenepass.com/blog/childcare-benefits-for-employees
Example: https://www.learningcaregroup.com/employer-solutions/

Form Partnerships with Local Churches
We will help churches to thrive in their communities, and reach new families through their kids, while creating new revenue streams. We will work to further the mission of the church by starting a preschool on the church premises. We will develop a questionnaire to assess how to best engage with the church, and assess the suitability of their facilities. We will pledge that students will also learn about Christian values that will help them develop into well-rounded individuals with happier lives, and a strong sense of morality and character. By partnering with the local church we will be able to ensure that the money otherwise spent on a lease, goes back into the work of the local church ministry and contributes to the profitability of the preschool business. We will initially negotiate the terms of the arrangement on a short-term basis, to evaluate the viability of the partnership. We will also save money by helping the church to directly market the preschool to their parishioners.

Source: https://www.youtube.com/watch?v=ucKlTGiiHQg
Resources: www.encouragepreschools.net/church-partnership-models/
               https://thepillarsclc.com/why-choose-a-christian-preschool-for-your-child/
               https://www.greatbeginningsaz.com/preschool-facility-requirements

XIX.   Referral Programs

Parent Referral Programs

We will use our parent referral program to offer incentives to parents, with children currently enrolled or graduated, to engage in word-of-mouth advertising, and generate new customers. We plan to offer various incentives to current customers to make recommendations and bring in other families.

Objective: To Turn Parents and Alumni into Marketing Sales Agents

Referral Program Preschool Benefits:
1.   Cost-effective way to lower customer acquisition costs
2.   Deepens customer loyalty, engagement and relationships
3.   Referral program application collects customer data.
4.   Use collected performance data to cross-sell other products and attract alliance partners.

Example: Quantas Loyalty Ventures
                www.qantas.com/au/en/about-us/our-company/subsidiary-companies.html
Qantas Loyalty is an innovative data led business that drives customer and partner loyalty through Qantas Frequent Flyer and Qantas Business Rewards programs. Members are rewarded with Qantas Points across a range of categories, including travel, financial services, retail, health and wellbeing insurance, food and wine, and small business services. At the heart of Qantas Loyalty is their data, marketing and analytics service, powered by Red Planet.

Customer Referral Reward Options:
1.   Money (Cash Payment)
2.   Gift Certificate for other businesses
3.   Discount on products or services
4.   Tuition credit or waived registration fee
5.   Physical product gift
6.   Free tickets to an event
7.   Donation to a charity
8.   Additional Reward: Give the referred family a bonus reward for attending
Note: The amount of the reward will be tied to the average cost of customer acquisition via other sales and marketing channels.

Parent Referral Payment Condition Options:

1. Take the tour (partial reward)
2. Officially sign registration form and make first payment
3. Wait until after the new customer has paid for at least three months.

Example of Graduated Referral Rewards Policy:
1. $50.00 paid for qualified lead and parent takes the tour.
2. $100.00 paid if parent signs enrollment agreement and makes initial payment.
3. $200.00 paid if child stays enrolled for at least one semester or year.

Track the Referral Process:
1. Ask referring parents to email notification of their referral with their contact information.
2. Create a form for referring parents to fill out.
3. Include a section in the application form for potential customers to note if someone referred them.
4. Create a spreadsheet to track all referral information, including the reward issuance date, amount, recipient and type.
5. Set a calendar reminder to send the reward.

Referral Software Resources:
https://referralrock.com/blog/small-business-referral-program/
https://www.zendesk.com/blog/customer-referral-program/#
https://viral-loops.com/referral-marketing-software

Referral Program Marketing Strategies
1. Distribute flyers or handouts to parents in on-boarding welcome and tour packages.
2. Include a section in the Parent Handbook or Consumer Guidebook
3. Document as a part of every email signature.
4. Describe the referral program in every issue of the newsletter.
5. Include newsletter articles about parents who have made successful referrals.
6. Send personalized reminders once per semester.
7. Post a sign in the lobby, or make a sidewalk sign.
8. Remind parents during private conversations.
9. Mention the program in the daily sheets and attach to student progress reports.
10. Create a contest to reward the parent with the most referrals each semester.
11. Celebrate referral milestones at preschool events.
12. Create a 'Referral Training Program', as a manual and video tutorial, for parents who want to pursue a new income opportunity.
13. Post a photo of the handing over the reward to social media accounts.
14. Conduct a drawing among the top 10 referral persons to win top prizes.

Examples: https://www.cadence-education.com/parent-referral/
https://kidsandcompany.com/programs/referral-program/
https://brightsideacademy.com/about-us/referral/
www.vipkid.com/login?prevUrl=%2Fmkt%2Frefer-center

Alumni Family Referral Program

This referral program will reward the referral actions of alumni families. Alumni will be required to fill-out an online Alumni Referral Form. They will receive a $ Gift Card and yearly recognition for our most valued referrers. In appreciation for the alumni referral, we will present a $200 book and stationery voucher for referral of every new (first-time) student, upon successful enrolment and full payment of school fees and all applicable charges for enrollment.

Examples: https://methodistpreschools.org/alumni-referral-programme-2024
                 https://gordon.tufts.edu/alumni/student-alumni-referral-program

Teacher Referral Program

We will develop a recruitment referral program as a hiring strategy where we will ask our existing employees to recommend or refer qualified teacher candidates who could be a good match for the company. It will be a way of expanding the talent pool without the need to reach out to outside sources. We will give referral program business cards to teachers so that they can get credit for recruiting teachers that remain on staff for at least ___ (6?) months.

Example: https://factorialhr.com/blog/employee-referral-programs/
Resource: https://resources.workable.com/stories-and-insights/employee-referral-program

XX.   Pricing Strategies

Conduct Annual Tuition Pricing Review

We will review pricing structures and competitor pricing strategies every 6 months. We will build annual price reviews into parent contracts to cover rising costs. We will explain the necessity to raise prices to be able to continue to offer quality services. We will justify the price increases by referencing the rising costs of teacher salaries, rent payments, tax increases, utilities costs and insurance premiums. We will also review the discounts being offered and discontinue those discounts to families who are not paying their fair share and/or are negatively impacting the financial health of our business.

Resources: https://trustedcare.com/costs/preschool-cost
https://blog.wonderschool.com/articles/tuition-pricing-strategies-for-in-home-child-care

Investigate Various Pricing Strategies

We will consider the pros and cons of the following pricing strategies:

1.   **Versioning Pricing**
      Offering different pricing tiers, by age group or service levels, such as for infants, and toddlers, because of higher teacher ratios, supply needs, and a greater level of care needed for younger-aged children.
2.   **Penetration Pricing**
      Rates are set at a low cost to attract first-time families for a limited time.
3.   **Value-Based Pricing**
      This is pricing that is tied to the value provided, such as healthy, organic, lunch meals.
4.   **Cost-Plus Pricing**

A desired profit margin is added to the actual cost-per-child in the program.

5. **Market Rate Pricing**

This pricing is derived from conducting competitor research and finding the average price being charged by local preschools with comparable services and facilities.

6. **Corporate Subsidized Pricing**

We will establish partnerships with corporations that want to subsidize tuition fees, as an employee benefit. Employees of these partner companies will receive discounted rates.

7. **Community Funding Model**

According to this model, local businesses and residents contribute to a common fund that supports the preschool. This approach not only helps to engage the community in the preschool, but also fosters a sense of shared neighborhood responsibility for early child learning. In some cases, a qualifying preschool must be a non-profit organization. Examples:

https://walmart.org/how-we-give/program-guidelines/spark-good-local-grants-guidelines
https://miamifoundation.org/2023-community-grants-partners/
www.thechildrenstrust.org/community-engagement-outreach-grants

8. **Subscription-based Pricing**

This allows parents to choose different levels of educational engagement and wraparound services for their children, from basic to premium, altering the cost accordingly.

9. **Sliding Scale Tuition Pricing**

This involves adjusting fees based on the family income, which is a model that promotes inclusivity. In this model, fees are proportionate to parental earnings, ensuring that no child is denied education due to cost.

10. **Grandfathered Pricing**

This involves raising pricing for currently enrolled families, at a reasonable rate of increase, and treating them as "Legacy Families" to create goodwill and retain existing customers. This strategy enables starting new enrollments at a higher rate to improve revenues at a faster rate.

Resource:
https://hingeadvisors.com/blog/the-true-cost-of-care-setting-your-preschool-tuition-rates
Directory:
https://childcare.gov/consumer-education/get-help-paying-for-child-care

Practice Premium Pricing

We will research the pricing strategies of our local competitors and establish a higher, all-inclusive, premium pricing policy. By charging this higher, distinctive branding pricing strategy, there will be a promise of no other charges. Everything will be included in our tuition fee.

We will include the following types of giveaway extras, which we will brand, and use as marketing tools:

1. Logo-imprinted uniforms and T-shirts to promote the school
2. Unlimited graduation tickets to drive community awareness and engagement.
3. Holiday family photos with school name captions.
4. School newsletter to advise of coming events and document milestone

accomplishments.
5.   Student portfolio folders, with school name cover, to hold student artwork.
6.   Parent attendance at school seminars and workshops to demonstrate and share staff expertise.
7.   Free copies of books self-published by expert preschool administrators on toddler social development best practices.

Establish a Parent Points Reward System

We will award parent points, or credits, which can be redeemed towards child tuition costs, if they engage in the following types of school supporting activities:
1.   Chaperone the students on a field trip.
2.   Contribute articles to the schools' monthly newsletter.
3.   Attend parent/teacher conferences.
4.   Share an education experience with a class, such as a music lesson.
5.   Attend school board meetings as a guest.
6.   Attend board officer development workshop.
7.   Hold board or committee member position for one year.
8.   Attend parent education or curriculum development meetings
9.   Participate in the planning and implementation of school holiday and fundraising events.
10.   Make a donation of more than $100.00 to a school fundraiser.
11.   Attend parent training workshops.
12.   Offer content or make presentations at parent training workshops.
13.   Attend orientation nights.
14.   Make parent/child referrals to the school.
15.   Make teacher/employee referrals to the school.
Resource:
https://www.sumnerco-oppreschool.org/current-families/parent-education-credits

XXI.   Pursue Location-based Growth Opportunities

We will research the competition and growth opportunities in neighborhoods and commercial areas that have families and persons who are a match to our ideal composite target market profile.

Possible pockets of opportunity for preschools include:
1.   **New Housing Developments:**
        Co-locating Affordable Housing and Preschools
        We will work with new affordable housing complexes to form partnerships, and determine if there are state tax incentives to incorporate an on-site preschool for the residents. These opportunities may involve the government and the private sector, collaborating to benefit local families. Our goal is to be located in the heart of the community, and be seen as a convenient complex amenity, for the residents, that

provides early learning or childcare opportunities.

Examples: www.khou.com/article/news/local/apartment-preschool-program-houston/
285-e45756dd-0a18-481b-a613-24f70613fa55

www.ksbe.edu/article/new-west-oahu-housing-development-will-include-on-site-preschool-funded-by-ks-kaiaulu

www.housingfinance.com/developments/preschool-working-families-share-one-roof_o

https://housingoregon.org/preschools-housing-integrating-early-childhood-learning-centers-in-affordable-housing-development/

Resource Types: County Housing Finance and Development Corporation
City Department of Education and Early Learning
State Housing Finance Commission

2.   **New Residents**
We will use the following tactics to target new movers to the area:
a.   Buy a mailing list of new movers from InfoUSA.com
b.   Advertise to new residents with 'WelcomeWagon.com'.
c.   Post flyers in new model homes.
d.   Form alliances with local Realtors and offer a special promotion.
    Directory: https://www.nar.realtor/directories
e.   Make a presentation to the local condo or apartment complex board.
f.   Provide discount coupons to local moving companies.
    Directory: https://www.moving.com/moving-companies-directory/
g.   Provide a sales package to relocation companies.
    Directory: https://vendordirectory.shrm.org/category/relocation
    https://www.worldwideerc.org/directory

3.   **New Business Complexes or Parks**
To help parents in the workforce with their childcare responsibilities, more employers are including child care in their benefit packages, and establishing childcare facilities within their worksites or complexes. Our goal is to be located in a business park so that parents can have convenient access to our preschool.
Examples: www.primroseschools.com/schools/highlands-ranch-business-park
https://child-care-preschool.brighthorizons.com/ma/franklin/franklin
https://learningvision.com/centres/learning-vision-changi-business-park/
Resource Types: Child Care Cooperatives owned and operated by their employees.

4.   **Shared New Construction Projects**
We will work with the experienced builders of childcare facilities, and research other businesses that want to service the same target market, and share or apportion the construction costs. Other types of business include: daycare, nursery school, infant care, childcare center, preschool program, after-school programs and summer camps.
Resource: https://mortonbuildings.com/projects/child-care
https://childcaredesign.com/a-state-by-state-breakdown-of-daycare-construction-costs/

5. **Consortium Model**
   We will assemble a consortium of multiple employers to establish new child care programs within our community.

XXII.   Preschool Parent Tours

Get More Parents to Take the Tour
We will use the following strategies to get more parents to take our facility tours:
1. Develop a phone script that collects the contact information from the caller, for follow-up purposes, and other decision-making criteria, such as required preschool attributes, and desired start date, budget parameters, and child name, age and interests.
2. Use the acquired parent and child information to personalize the tour experience.
3. Introduce the concept of scarcity by advising that there are only a limited number of open spots available for the coming term.
4. Advise parents of an expiring special offer, and what it will take to qualify and benefit from the special deal.
5. Train phone answerers to highlight the preschool competitive advantages, that are important to the caller, based on their statement of needs and wants.
6. Promote the taking of the tour as a means to also experience a free consultation about early childcare learning options.
7. Enable parents to self-service the booking or scheduling of a tour, via a calendar available on the preschool website.
   Resource:
   https://blog.lineleader.com/drive-higher-enrollment-rates-with-parent-scheduled-tours
8. Automatically send a confirmation email, upon tour booking, with the tour time, preschool name and address, multiple Director contact options, and Thank you note.
9. Hand-out logo-imprinted favors for taking the tour, like a small educational toy or copy of the Director's self-published book about the secrets to raising behavior challenged toddlers.
10. Offer to include a free parenting consultation to share acquired toddler expertise.
11. Advise parents that they welcome to bring their child, who may want to participate in a classroom activity.

Resource: www.daycarestudio.net/home/how-to-give-an-amazing-tour-parents-cant-refuse

Develop a Tour Checklist for Parents
We will develop a tour checklist for parents to help them to ask the right questions and make an informed enrollment decision:

Does the preschool have an acceptable or low teacher/student ratio?
Are parents welcome to visit without an appointment?
Do the teachers have adequate educations, backgrounds, and/or certified credentials?
Do teachers communicate with parents about daily school happenings?

Do the teachers generate monthly student progress reports?
Does the preschool have a written policy for discipline when behavior issues arise?
Is there someone on staff who is trained to handle medical needs?
What is the educational philosophy of the preschool (Montessori, Waldorf, Reggio Emilia)?
Does the preschool have a sick child policy?
Does the preschool have a personal wellness plan for the children?
Does the preschool have adequate facility access protections?
Does the preschool have adequate safety, security, and emergency procedures in place to protect the children?
Does the preschool have an active state license to operate?
Does the preschool provide nutritious meals?
Does the preschool accommodate children with allergies or dietary restrictions?
Does the preschool offer any afterschool enrichment programs?
Are the preschool's operating hours a match to your needs?
Are the rates in line with competitor research?
Does the preschool have a vaccinations policy?
Does the preschool have a birthday celebration policy?
Does the preschool teach cultural diversity?
Do teachers interact with the children in a caring way?
Are the classroom materials and outdoor equipment safe and in good condition?
Do the kids have opportunities for hands-on learning activities?
Does the class follow a flexible schedule each day?
Are there opportunities for children to play outside?
Can the children make their own choices for activity participation?
Do teachers use multiple teaching methods?
Do teachers accommodate students who need special assistance?
Do the teachers have special procedures for handling misbehaving children?
Have the teachers been trained to facilitate the motor skills and social development of the children?
Does the preschool adequately train children for kindergarten?
Does the preschool make available an adequate number of parent reviews or references?

Source: https://winnie.com/resources/checklist-for-touring-a-preschool
               https://mybrightwheel.com/blog/5-things-to-ask-on-a-preschool-tour-2

Master the Science of Curb Appeal

We will pursue the following strategies to make an outstanding first impression from the street, and turn our curb appeal into a WOW factor:

1.   Colorful, lite signage, that is, not only attached to the face of the building, but is also perpendicular to it, and incorporated into window and sidewalk signage.
2.   A manicured landscape that features freshly mowed grass, trimmed trees and flowering plants.
3.   The playground has a focus on child safety, with extensive use of artificial turf, rubberized flooring materials, foam padding and child-proof fencing.

4. All playground toys are clean, refurbished and/or are in good working order.
5. Exterior fencing, and window and door trims are freshly painted, and easy to maintain and keep clean.
6. Colorful exterior lighting that is not only eye-catching, but also promotes safety.
7. A parking lot that is kept clean and free of potholes, and features video surveillance cameras and nighttime flood-lighting, to help visitors feel safe.
8. Sidewalks are swept and power-washed, on a weekly basis, and be well-maintained for safety reasons.
9. Remove any smudges or fingerprints from glass windows and doors.
10. All trash and debris have been collected and removed from the property.
12. The front door advises of the access safety protocols.

Ready the Preschool for Tours

1. Clean the school with a lemon-scented cleaner, and connect a fragrant air diffuser to the central ventilation system.
2. Play soft, calming music in the background.
3. Remove all clutter and debris from the building.
4. Place a copy of the class schedule and curriculum on the bulletin board next to the classroom door.
5. Prepare the teachers to showcase an in-progress class and welcome a visiting potential student and parent to experience the class.
6. Check the operation of all student security and safety measures.
7. Show off the video surveillance system and how-to gain access to it.
8. Assemble the contents of the registration sales portfolio or enrollment package.
9. Block off an adequate period of time to conduct the tour.
10. Place a welcome sign on the front door with the visiting parent and child names.
11. Prepare and offer a selection of healthy snacks and beverages.
12. Create tour stops that highlight the preschool's core values and mission statement, such as a classroom with well-behaved children who are learning-by-doing, in a culturally-diverse, small group setting.

Resources:
https://hingeadvisors.com/blog/childcare-center-tour-secrets-and-strategies
www.childcaresuccess.com/back-to-basics-little-things-to-have-in-place-during-a-tour-to-
    wow-parents/

Assemble a Sales Package for the Tour
We will assemble both a e-Packet and a hardcopy version of our sales presentation portfolio, and include the following items:
1. Owner or Founder Backstory
2. Letter from the Preschool Director with multiple contact options.
3. Teacher Bio's and Condensed Resumes of the Admin Team.
4. The Preschool's Unique Value Proposition
5. Preschool Evaluation Checklist to show confidence and expertise.
6. Copy of Referral Program with incentives that encourage word-of-mouth advertising.

7.	Tour Booking Incentives, Process and Topic Highlights
8.	Common Questions and Answers
9.	Reprints of Local Media Coverage
10.	Parent Testimonials and Academic Reviews
11.	Article Reprints about 'Child Social Development'.
12.	Tips for Choosing the Right Preschool with competitor comparisons
13.	Layout Diagram of the Preschool
14.	Sample Student Registration Form
15.	Sample of Proposed Curriculum
16.	Sample of Student Progress Report
17.	Sample Copy of Monthly e-Newsletter
18.	Overview of the Preschool Industry: Benefits, Trends and Data
19.	Calendar of Scheduled Preschool Events
20.	Parent Needs Assessment Questionnaire
21.	Program Information Page with fee schedule, teacher/student ratios, operating hours, education philosophy and call-to-action.
22.	List of things students need to bring to the preschool, including snacks, clothes, supplies, diapers, sippy cup, etc.
23.	List of student safety measures, and room and toy cleaning procedures.
24.	Provide a swag gift bag with logo-imprinted items, such as a T-shirt.

Resources:
https://visme.co/blog/sales-pitch-presentation-template/
https://www.hopkinsmedicine.org/health/wellness-and-prevention/10-must-ask-questions-and-tips-on-choosing-a-preschool

Present Competitive Advantages on the Tour
1.	State-of-the-art outdoor playground
2.	Outdoor equipment selected based on safety criteria, and to improve gross motor skills and student interaction.
2.	Uniquely designed indoor imagination playroom, that is also available for private parties and weekend playdates.
3.	A niche focus on academic development and readiness for grammar school grades.

Develop Proper Tour Giving Skills
We will develop a program to train the preschool Directors on how-to deliver an outstanding tour experience for parents.
1.	Make the theme of the tour to extend an invitation to the family to enroll and join the preschool community.
2.	Ask the parent to fill-out a Parent Needs Assessment Survey to gain a better understanding of the family's demographic profile and the parent's needs and wants for their child's development.
3.	Instruct the parent on how-to use our Parent Tour Checklist
4.	Address the parent and child by their names.
5.	Demonstrate how the preschool can provide solutions to the needs that that family is expressing.

6. Convey a sense of open communication and transparency.
7. Explain the many ways in which the child will benefit from being enrolled at the school.
8. Incorporate encouraging calls-to-action throughout the tour and enrollment processes.
9. If a family isn't ready to enroll during the tour, offer to follow up with them and make sure to keep any promises made.

Post the Tour Routine

We will develop the following post tour routine:
1. Send the parent a handwritten thank you note for taking the tour
2. Follow-up with a call in 2 to 3 days to answer any new questions.
3. Add the parent captured information to the CRM database for drip-marketing purposes.
4. Send a post-tour survey that asks for tour comments and factors that are influencing the making of a final decision.

Assemble an Open House Kit

We will assemble an open house kit with the following contents:
1. A step-by-step hosting agenda with timetable
2. Email and printed invitation templates
3. Thank you note cards
4. Welcome wall banner
5. Marketing materials templates
6. List of recommended educational games and toys
7. Description of art projects
8. Assortment of coloring pages
9. Parent directions for preparing children for classes
10. Preschool location and community maps
11. List of suggested snacks and beverages
12. Teacher tour guide badges
13. Teacher resume templates
14. Parent sign-in sheets
15. Outline for family information guide
16. Sample parent questions and answers
17. Sample enrollment form
18. Price list template
19. Sample logo-imprinted giveaway item
20. Curriculum outline with sample materials

Source: www.thingstoshareandremember.com/hosting-a-preschool-open-house/

Run More Open House Events

We will run more open house events, on a quarterly basis, to accomplish the following objectives:
1. Share the educational philosophy of the preschool with the community.
2. Increase the visibility of the school.
3. Welcome parent accompanied children to experience classroom activities.
4. Encourage more parents to sign-up for tours and consultations.

We will create an operations plan for the holding of open house events, and it will include the following elements:

1. Choose a date and time that does not conflict with other community or local school events, and avoid holidays and weekends.
2. Train Staff Greeters and teachers, how-to welcome attendees and explain the educational philosophy of the preschool.
3. Ask teachers to participate in these events who are more outgoing and likely to strike up conversations with prospective parents, and have the knowledge to answer a parent's questions and respond to objections.
4. Assign an open house event manager who will be responsible for running the event, collecting and tabulating parent surveys, and tracking the relevant performance metrics, including the number of attendees and their information source.
5. Establish event themes, goals, responsibilities, timetable, plans and budget.
6. Develop an event marketing plan using Facebook, Parent Meet-up Groups, Neighborhood Online Groups, Company Website Open House Event Sign-up Button, Instagram flyer photos, outdoor signage, press releases, etc.
7. Provide referral type incentives for enrolled parents to send or bring prospective families to the open house event.
8. Decorate classrooms with welcome signs, and student art and lesson plans.
9. Build a healthy snack and beverage dispensing table.
10. Set up a table with crafts or educational toys, in a part of the classroom, where the children can be supervised, and kept occupied with independent play activities.
11. Highlight all of the health, safety and security measures taken by the preschool.
12. Assemble sales portfolios, including brochures, enrollment packets, sample schedules, calendars, sample student progress reports, FAQ resources, family reviews, list of competitive advantages, and family handbooks, as handouts to be given to parents.
13. Conducts tours of the complete preschool, and be prepared to answer commonly asked questions.
14. Highlight activities that are designed to foster student social development and creativity.
15. Let the children participate in both indoor and outdoor activities, so they have options to choose from.
16. Encourage attending families to submit their enrollment applications by offering an exclusive incentive, such as a tuition discount or waived registration fee.
17. Develop and implement an attendee follow-up, drip-marketing program, that includes an email with: Preschool brochure, parent testimonials, thank you note for attending event, survey to gather event feedback, parent handbook and school policies, and contact information.
18. Set up an information table and use greeters to distribute sample schedules, brochures, enrollment information and family handbooks.

Source: https://www.preschool-plan-it.com/open-house.html
https://mybrightwheel.com/blog/open-house-childcare-preschool
https://blog.wonderschool.com/articles/9-must-dos-for-a-successful-preschool-open-house-event

Resource: https://illumine.app/blog/how-to-host-a-fun-preschool-open-house-to-boost-admission-rates/

Flyer Content:
Come tour our preschool facilities, meet our staff and learn more about our curriculum and learn-by-doing programs, at our upcoming Open House Event.
Registering now for Spring/Fall/Summer/Winter ____ (year) programs.
When: Weekday Evening, _____ Date, from 6 p.m. to 9 p.m.
Where: Location Address
For inquiries or to pre-register for the Open House Event, please email __or call ___

Master Student Assessments to Show Results
We will conduct early childhood education assessments by gathering information about a child to evaluate their knowledge, monitor their progress, evaluate readiness for the next grade and guide educational instruction. We will use the following methods for assessment, to help convince parents that they are making a wise investment in the academic and social development of their children:

Progress Report Cards
Portfolio of Work Samples
Social Interaction Observations
Problem Solving Observations
Learning Observations
One-to-One Conversations
Educator Ratings
Child Achievement Reviews
Parent Ratings
Kindergarten Readiness Tests
Kindergarten Entry Assessments (KEAs)
Other Standardized Tests
Summative Assessment Tools
Resource: https://mybrightwheel.com/blog/formal-vs-informal-assessment
https://illumine.app/blog/writing-effective-preschool-assessment-reports-a-quick-guide/

Create a Thank You Gift Package for Taking the Tour
We will develop a gift package or goodie bag with items that have been branded with eye-catching labels that contain our preschool name, phone number and website address. We will include a mix of the following items to thank parents for taking our tour, build a sense of goodwill, and as a means of staying top-of-mind:

1.   The above referenced sales package.
2.   Merchandise branded with the school's logo, including T-shirt, mug, calendar, sippy cups, water bottles, tote bag, onesie, hats, bibs, bag clips, bubbles, etc.
3.   Educational items, such as children's books, educational toys, games and toys.
4.   Arts and crafts items, such as themed coloring books, crayons, colored markers, etc.

Create an End-of-Tour Ritual
1. Thank the parent for filling out the parent needs assessment form and taking the time to fully experience the tour.
2. Formally handover the sales package and the gift package.
3. Ask if any other questions need to be answered.
4. Provide multiple contact options.
5. Confirm that the child would be a good fit for the preschool.
6. Ask for the enrollment.

Establish a Follow-up Program
1. Send a handwritten note thanking the parent for taking the tour with enclosed business card and favorite school poem
2. In subsequent days, launch a structured follow-up drip marketing campaign, using email, text messages, and phone calls to stay-in-touch.
3. Assemble a personalized direct mail package with flyers, newsletter copies, special event invitation from the preschool director, parent testimonials, parent questionnaire to surface any remaining issues or concerns, and/or a coupon for a free trial attendance day at the preschool.

Resources:
ChildcareCRM   https://lineleader.com/feature/marketing-automation
Automatically sends stored email and text templates. Uses dynamic content to engage families with personalization keys like their first name, and child's name.

Meritto   www.meritto.com/crm-software-for-preschools-and-child-day-care/
A unified CRM for preschools to attract, engage and enroll more students.

XXIII.   Offer Preschool Program Package Options
We will give parents the option of paying an all-inclusive or premium tuition fee, with included wraparound services, or unbundle the products and services to charge a basic tuition fee and add extras on an as wanted ala carte basis.

Unbundle the package and charge optional separate fees for each of the following services:

		Examples:
1.	Early drop-off fees	$40/month between 6:30am-8:30am
2.	Late pick-up fees	$5.00/minute
3.	Number of Days per week	1 to 5 Days per week
		4 Days a Week Preschool Only - $1000/Month
4.	Half Day Program Blocks	8:45am Drop-Off to 11:45am Pick-Up
		2 Day a week Preschool – $350/month
5.	Flexible Daycare Coverage	

6.	After School Transportation fees	$20.00
7.	Field trip fees	$25.00
8.	Additional Breakfast Meal fee	$2.00
9.	Traditional Lunch Fee	$3.00
9.	Organic Hot Lunch fee	$5.00
10.	Snack Fees	Food-service: meal-ala-carte-prices
11.	Holiday Daycare fee	
12.	Part-time Daycare fee	
13.	Summer Camps fees	$90.00/day.... $400.00/week
14.	Portfolio presentation folder	
15.	Live Streaming fee	
16.	Photography fees	Print package cost is $50.00
		Digital file fee is $40.00
17.	Parent Seminar Event fees	Free for enrolled families/
		$25.00 for non-registered parents
18.	Graduation Ticket fees	$30.00
19.	Graduation Gown Rental fee	$25.00
20.	Afterschool Enrichment Pgm	$400.00/month $110.00/week
21.	Waitlist / Application Fee	$125.00/child
22.	Initial Enrollment Fee	$300.00 first child $200.00 Subsequent
23.	Annual Re-enrollment Fee	$200.00 first child $100.00 Subsequent
24.	One-time textbook fee	$50.00
25.	Return Check Fee	$30.00
26.	Late Payment Fee	$20.00/day
27.	Supply Fee	$35.00 (per child per school year)

Examples: https://turtlerockpreschool.com/admissions/tuition/
https://www.sothpreschool.com/fee-schedule

Unbundle the Package and Charge Separate Fees for Products/Supplies
1. Extra Supplies: Pampers, Wipes, etc.
2. Healthy Snacks
Source: www.nitrocollege.com/blog/extra-expenses-daycare

Develop a Parent Needs Assessment Questionnaire
We will use a portion of the tour to ask parent to complete our Prospective Parent Needs Assessment Questionnaire. The purpose of the survey will be to determine and prioritize the preschool offerings that are more important to the individual parents.

Instructions: Please elaborate upon each of the following preschool selection considerations, and assign a priority weight factor, from 1 to 10, with 10 indicating very important:

Parent Name	Parent Contact Info
Child Name	Child Age
Child Allergies	Child Hobbies
Child Likes	Child Challenges

	Description	Priority 1 - 10
1.	Child Safety	
2.	Respect for Cultural Diversity	
3.	Open Lines of Communication	
4.	Multiple Communication Methods	
5.	Admin Inquiry Responsiveness	
6.	Established Emergency Procedures	
7.	Environment Friendliness	
8.	Access to Support Groups/Services	
9.	Parent Involvement Welcomed	
10.	Classroom Video Monitoring	
11.	Regular Parent-Teacher Conferences	
12.	Facility and Toy Cleanliness	
13.	Teacher Certifications	
14.	Teacher Consistency	
15.	Student to Teacher Ratio	
16.	Solutions to Parenting Challenges	
17.	Agreement with Disciplinary Approach	
18.	Healthiness of the Food Menu	
19.	Challenge Level of Curriculum	
20.	Kindergarten Readiness	
21.	Achievement of Other Child Goals	
22.	Offer English Learner Program	
23.	Availability of Parent Seminars	
24.	Availability of Special Needs Resources	
25.	Agreement with Educational Philosophy	
26.	All-inclusive Pricing	

Open-ended Questions for Parents:
1. What are you primarily looking for in a preschool program?
2. What concerns or challenges do you want help addressing with your child:
   - Potty training
   - Eating habits
   - Behavioral issues
   - Social development
   - Gross Motor Skills
   - Special Needs
   - Other
3. What preschool goals do you have for your child over the next year or two?

Resources:
https://calpella.uusd.net/apps/pages/index.jsp?uREC_ID=794884&type=d&pREC_ID=1186617
https://parentsinc.org/spedpac/assessment.html
https://www.teacherspayteachers.com/browse?search=preschool%20parent%20questionnaire

XXIV.   Actively Solicit Parent Feedback

Solicit Parent Feedback for Continuous Improvement

We will develop the following Preschool Parent Survey to semi-annually gather parent feedback, that will help the preschool to surface and address hidden issues, and continuously make improvements:

1. Overall Preschool Program Grade: A/B/C/D/F
2. Would you recommend the Preschool to friends and relatives?
3. Are you happy with your child's academic/social development progress?
4. Is your child happy with the learning program?
5. Are you happy with the academic and licensing credentials of the teachers and administers?
6. Are the teachers and director involved in ongoing training or continuing education programs?
7. How satisfied are you with the helpfulness of your child's teachers?
8. How would you rate the quality of interaction your child receives from their teachers.
9. Are you happy with how often the teachers communicate about your child's progress?
10. Who is your favorite teacher or team member?   ......Why?
11. Who is your least favorite teacher or team member?   ...... Why?
12. Is your child realizing the desired level of independence and self-confidence?
13. Has your child's ability to socialize with other children improved?
14. Does the preschool provide opportunities to meet other families in the community?
15. Circle all the child needs that the curriculum satisfies: academic/physical/emotional
16. Do you find the classrooms to be clean, well-decorated, fully-equipped and organized?
17. Do you find the playground to be safe, well-organized, and well-equipped?
18. What do you especially like about your child's classroom?
19. What do you dislike about your child's classroom?
20. Does the food program meet the nutritional needs and dietary restrictions of your child?
21. Are you happy with the child check-in and check-out procedures?
22. Are you happy with the emergency plan in case a child is injured, sick, or lost?
23. Are you happy with the types of technology used to support the program?
24. Are there enough clean toys and learning materials for the number of children?
25. Is there a good daily balance of play time, story time, activity time, and nap time?
26. Did you receive a copy of the Parent Handbook prior to enrollment?
27. Do you have any issues with the enrollment contract you were asked to sign?
28. Did the program clearly outline the cost of care, field trip or special program fees, and any other fees?
29. Rate the preschool environment from 1 to 10 in each of the following areas:
    ___ Safety ___ Nurturing ___ Stimulating ___ Learning ___ Social Development
30. Rate from 1 to 10 how well the curriculum is aligned with the child's developmental needs and interests.
31. Rate from 1 to 10 the availability of resources to enhance parenting skills and knowledge.
32. Rate from 1 to 10 your perceived reputation and brand image of the preschool.
33. Were you explained the policy regarding termination of your child care agreement?

34. How would rate the implementation of the suggestions submitted by parents in prior surveys?
35. Comments:

Example: https://www.gfumc.com/preschool-parent-survey
Source: www.childcareaware.org/families/choosing-quality-child-care/selecting-child-care-program/preschool-program-checklist/

Act Upon Parent Feedback
To improve the growth potential of our preschool, we will pursue the following tactics:
1. Compile the results of the surveys.
2. Develop a plan-of-action based on the information conveyed by parents in their feedback surveys.
3. Post the plan to the website blog and company e-newsletter to convince parents that the school takes their feedback very seriously.
4. Keep parents informed as to the implementation status of the improvement plan.
5. Ask the parent, in subsequent surveys, to supply feedback, as to the positive impact of the implemented suggestions.

XXV.   Provide Parent School Selection Guidance

Help Parents to Make the Right Preschool Choice
We will demonstrate our confidence in the quality of our preschool by helping parents to make the informed preschool comparisons, and registration decisions. We will develop the following template to help parents to collect pertinent, decision-informing information:

Calendar entries will include:

	Preschool #1	Preschool #2	Preschool #3
Visitation hours			
Open house dates			
Application deadlines			
Observation visits			
Interviews			

Family and Parent Friend Recommendations:

Name	Preschool Preference	Reason

Online Research Sources:

	Preschool	Findings
Google		
Facebook		
TripAdvisor		

Community Space Interviews:
Neighborhood Playgrounds
Religious Institutions
MeetUp.com Groups

School Visits:

Preschool Name	Contact	Curriculum	Program	Cost	Fit Assessment

Program Types:	Pros	Cons	Net
Montessori			
Waldorf			
HighScope			
Co-Ops			
Bank Street			
Reggio Emilia			

Create Smart Consumers of Preschool Programs

We will give parents a copy of the following questionnaire to demonstrate our self-confidence in the selection process and to help parents to make better-informed preschool contracting decisions for their children:
1. Are you properly licensed by the appropriate local authorities?
2. Do you have a safe environment with appropriate supervision?
3. How does the school ensure the cleanliness of the facility and toys?
4. What policies are in place and precautions used to ensure my child's well-being?
5. How do you deal with behavioral issues?
6. How will I be informed if my child is disciplined?
7. How large will my child's class be?
8. What is the staff-to-child ratio?
9. What time does preschool begin and end?
10. Are before- and/or after-care offered?
12. Is the preschool open during holidays and/or summers?
13. Are there an open-lines-of-communication with directors and teachers?
14. Who do I go to with my concerns and questions?
15. What activities are offered on a typical day?
16. What is the teaching philosophy of the preschool?
17. What food, in terms of meals and snacks, are provided for my child?
18. Does my child need to be toilet trained or partly toilet trained, and at what age?
19. Is there rest or nap time each day, and if so, at what time(s) and for how long?
20. How much does it cost, and what does this cost include?
21. Does the preschool offer individualized learning or support for children with special needs?
22. In what ways can parents be involved in the education process?
23. What is the plan to develop the child's gross motor skills?
Resource: https://www.ourkids.net/school/questions-to-ask-preschools

XXVI.   Document Student Progress

Assemble Child Portfolios to Show Progress

We will assemble child portfolios to document and showcase the unique accomplishments and the developmental progress of each child in our preschool program. Tracking children's development with a portfolio will support and show proof of learning outcomes, improve family engagement, and allow the preschool administrators to evaluate the effectiveness of each program. It will provide a record of each child's development and contain important milestones, such as the important skills learned, the ways learning occurs, and how the child interacts with their peers and environment. The portfolio will be a digital collection of individual student records or a physical portfolio, or a combination of both.

Typical contents will include:
1. Photographs of the child engaging in activities
2. Video recordings or descriptions of conversations with the child
3. Recommendations and observations from teachers
4. Writing and art samples, and drawings.
5. Documentation of the stages of the child's developmental progress
6. Copies of the child's progress reports.
7. Attendance record.
8. Behavioral problem documentation.

Source: www.procaresoftware.com/blog/how-to-make-a-child-care-portfolio/
Resources:
https://mybrightwheel.com/blog/3-tips-to-make-curating-child-care-portfolios-easier

XXVII.   Onboarding Services

We will develop distinctive onboarding strategies for parents, teachers and students because they will present our first opportunity to make a positive first impression.

Parent Onboarding Programs
1. Provide a Welcome Packet, Parent Handbook and Parent Orientation Class that covers drop-off and pick-up procedures, curriculum overview, tuition policies and events calendar.
2. Establish a parent community to help parents to get to know each other.
3. Offer a walking tour of the center and make introductions to admin staffers and teachers.
4. Set-up assigned teacher meet-and-greets with parents.
5. Discuss child safety and security measures.

6. Allow for question-and-answer sessions and relevant topic discussions and debates in an open forum.
   Resource: https://mailchimp.com/resources/how-to-create-a-forum-website/
7. Forward to parents a document that summarizes what was covered by the orientation class.
8. Make an ACH agreement part of the onboarding process for new parents by putting an ACH authorization form into the tuition agreement.
9. Develop a registration application that helps to develop insightful profiles of both the parent and student, in terms of the child's health issues, values, interests, talents, and challenges, the parent's concerns, objectives and goals.
   Examples: www.jotform.com/form-templates/preschool-registration-2
                      https://childcarelounge.com/pages/free-child-care-forms-printable-reports-letters-contracts
10. Produce videos that describe the student orientation, and learning philosophies and methodologies.
11. Produce videos that show parents how they can encourage and support student learning outside the classroom, and the specific roles that parents can play.
    Example: BeyondSkool   www.youtube.com/watch?v=1wJ1GWCjegk
12. Send out invitations to celebrate a customary yearly orientation day celebration.
13. Develop a 'Parent Orientation Program' that familiarizes parents with the preschool's policies, procedures, and expectations, including information about attendance, dress code, discipline, progress reports, extracurricular activities, etc.
14. Provide resources for parents where they can find more early childcare learning, nutrition and disciplinary information, and be ready to point them in the right direction, when necessary.
Resource: https://mybrightwheel.com/blog/childcare-preschool-orientation-ideas

Employee/Teacher Onboarding Program
1. Provide a Welcome Letter and introduce the Employee Handbook.
2. Host a new hire orientation day event to enable the building of relationships with co-workers and management.
3. Invite the preschool director to speak about the company's core values, culture, mission and vision statements, and desired brand image.
4. Provide a tour of the facilities and plan for group activities.
5. Enable new staffers to shadow an experienced teacher for several months, and assign them to a mentor and specific problem-solving teams.
6. Host a welcoming gathering of all teachers in the conference room or library.
7. Develop a mentoring program and assign the new hire to an experienced mentor.
8. Set up weekly check-ins to gather feedback.
9. Provide multiple ways for new hires to communicate and connect with families.
10. Acquaint the new hires with the preschool's marketing strategies, and the roles they can play.
11. Establish access to video training programs and assigned account login.
12. Provide the new hire with the section of the Operations Manual that pertains to their duties and responsibilities, and reporting interfaces.
13. Use the employment application to uncover employee likes, dislikes, hobbies, and

favorite foods, beverages and restaurants, to customize rewards and incentives.
14. Take new hires to lunch to celebrate their 30-day and one-year anniversaries, and gather direct feedback.
15. Develop daily, weekly, monthly and quarterly checklists for reoccurring and regulation mandated tasks, and assign persons responsible.
16. Create structured binders for new hires to organize information about parent visits and student assessments.
17. Acquaint new hires with the availability and access to training and mentorship programs and other types of resources.

Resources: https://mybrightwheel.com/blog/onboarding-new-childcare-staff
www.childcarebizhelp.com/childcare-employee-onboarding-process/
https://kangarootime.com/blog/free-childcare-staff-onboarding-checklist
https://trainual.com/template/childcare-center-new-employee-onboarding-process

Child Onboarding Checklist
1. Obtain child emergency contact information.
2. Add caregiver contact info to the communication database.
3. Document any child special needs, allergies and dietary requirements.
4. Assign Cubbie space and post identifying child photo.
5. Organize the child's supplies in their assigned Cubbie space.
6. Assign an art portfolio slot for child artwork.
7. Forward child background profile to the assigned teacher.
8. Introduce the new student to the class with a warm welcome by the existing students.
9. Assign the child to a buddy or small group, on a rotating basis, to foster a spirit of collaboration.
Resource: https://www.lillio.com/templates/new-child-onboarding-checklist

Alumni Onboarding Checklist
1. Ask alumni to enter their profile into the online alumni directory.
2. Ask alumni to sign-up for participation in coming events.
3. Coach alumni and their parents on how-to contribute to the marketing campaign as a brand ambassador or influencer.
4. Explain the referral and recognition programs for contributions of time and money to the preschool.

Preschool Welcome Packet
The welcome packet will include the following items:
1. Preschool Director and Teacher Welcome Letters
2. School Calendar
3. Daily Schedule
4. School Supply List
5. Instructions as to when to keep a sick child at-home.
6. Acceptable Child Dress Code
7. A List of Common Preschool Parent Concerns by age group and how the school will handle the situations.

8. A Handbook of School Rules for parents
9. Recommended Hygiene Procedures for parents to practice with their child at home.
10. Parent and Student Profile Forms
11. Address Mailing Labels
12. List of All School Contacts
13. Curriculum Overview with Educational Philosophy
14. Parent to-do Checklist
15. Overview of the School's Meal Program
16. Classroom Rules
17. Photo Release Form
18. Branded T-shirt and Refrigerator Magnet with Contact Options

Source: https://preschool.org/preschool-welcome-packet/
www.etsy.com/market/preschool_welcome_packets?ref=cq_tag_bottom_text-7

Resources:
https://www.teacherspayteachers.com/Product/My-Entire-Preschool-Welcome-Packet-7094336?st=6805fbae6a17b58d00bd424a313baa7d
https://modernpreschool.com/product/welcome-back-school-pack/

XXVIII. Launch Fee-based Consulting Services

Homeschooling Consultancy

We will take the knowledge that we have accumulated from our preschool business, and use it to create a homeschooling consultancy. We will assemble an Operations Manual that provides lots of helpful information on how to homeschool preschool children. This consultancy will not only provide another revenue stream, but also raise our profile within the community. We may also develop a revenue stream from the sales and rental of equipment (tables/chairs), educational toys and games, and children's books, and from the sales of supplies to homeschooling parents. We will also charge homeschoolers to attend our field trips and other school events. We will also share our knowledge of IQ Tests for children, which can provide an indication of a child's natural inclination towards a certain subject.

Fact: About 3.1 million students or 6% of school-age children are homeschooled.

Source: www.nheri.org/how-many-homeschool-students-are-there-in-the-united-states-during-the-2021-2022-school-year/

Resource: https://iq-tests.org/iq-test-for-kids.html

We will cover the following topics:

1. The State's homeschooling requirements
2. How to determine the child's preferred learning style
3. How to decide on a curriculum and lesson plan options
4. How to establish learning objectives.
5. How to create a homeschooling schedule

6. How to calculate homeschooling costs
7. How to monitor the child's progress
8. How to incorporate fun into the program.

Resources: www.time4learning.com/how-to/homeschool-preschool.html
               www.homeschool.com/articles/how-to-homechool-your-preschooler/
Preschool Homeschool Curriculum Directory:
               www.splashlearn.com/blog/preschool-homeschool-curriculum/

Montessori Homeschooling Consultancy

We will consult parents on how to support their child's development, with a focused
Montessori education approach, that helps to build independence and self-confidence
through practical and creative home-based activities and exercises. We will focus on
presenting hands-on activities that are tied to children's natural interests. We will offer
authentic Montessori curriculum planning programs and suggested daily schedules. We
will link every activity to a specific toddler age group. We will also provide a list of all
the materials needed for each activity.

Example: https://www.montessorielements.com/consultancy
Resource: https://printables.montessorinature.com/new-to-montessori-
               homeschooling/

Sales of Customized Homeschooling Curriculum Kits

We will assemble bespoke collections of curriculum materials that meet the specific
needs of individual homeschoolers. We will also offer these complete grade-level
curriculum products, as part of a subscription service.

Directory: https://www.homeschool.com/top10/top10reviews-asp/
               www.verywellfamily.com/best-online-homeschool-programs-4842632
               https://blog.quickschools.com/2023/12/07/top-10-best-online-accredited-
               homeschool-programs-for-2023/
Example: https://timberdoodle.com/collections/curriculum-kits?page=1
Resource:
National Home Education Research Institute
               www.nheri.org/research-facts-on-homeschooling/

Preschool Parenting Consultancy

Our preschool parenting consultancy will develop multiple Preschool Parenting
Programs, from basic to advanced. The objective will be to strengthen parent-child
interactions and attachment, reducing the need for excessive discipline and fostering
parents' ability to promote children's social, emotional, and language development.
Parents will also be coached on how to build school readiness skills, and promote
children's emotional regulation and social skills. The advanced parenting program
will focus on parents' interpersonal issues, such as child emotional support and anger
management.

Example: www.incredibleyears.com/early-intervention-programs/parents/preschoolers

Home Playroom Design Consultancy

We will design home playroom spaces for child development by creating custom spaces where children will love to learn, play and reset. All of our designers will be former teachers who know how to engage children in purposeful play, based on a specific educational philosophy. As an example, playrooms designed according to the Montessori method will be organized and designed to encourage independence and possess a simplicity of design philosophy. Our spaces will be designed to stimulate all senses, including touch, sight, hearing and movement. Our goal will be to create educational and child-centered playrooms, that are customized to the ages and interests of the families' children, while simultaneously stimulating open-ended, creative, thought-provoking play, and inspiring imaginations and active physical play. We will create spaces that are child safe, age and stage appropriate, and functional and well-organized.

We will provide two design service delivery options. We will offer a virtual custom design service, where we will send digital files, including 3D renders, clickable shopping lists and CAD drawings for the build out. Alternatively, we will offer a bespoke custom design service where we will work with the client every step of the way, including measuring, designing, purchasing and project managing. This option will also include ongoing consulting via phone or on-site, and design revisions. We will also establish affiliate marketing relationships with the equipment and supply manufacturers, and collect referral commissions from product sales.

Preferred Types of Toys:
1. Educational
2. Made of Natural, Sustainable Materials
3. Textured Finishes
4. Colorful
5. Easy-to-Clean

Typical Design Elements:

Play Kitchen	Play Grocery Store
Storage Cubbies	Storage Cabinets
Storage Baskets	Low Storage Bins
Closet Organization	Arts and Craft Station
Crafting Workbench	Table and Chairs
Reading Nook	Reading Lamp
Bookcases	Hanging Rack Systems
Wall Art	Wall Stickers/Decals
Area Rug	Toy Chest
Bean Bags	Bench Seating
Magnetic Board	Chalkboard
Whiteboard	

Examples: https://www.smartplayrooms.com/
https://grohplayrooms.com/team
https://www.smartplayrooms.com/pages/bespoke-design

Child Home Environment Consultancy

Our goal will be to create safe and well-organized physical conditions, opportunities for children to play-to-learn, and introduce developmentally appropriate objects, toys and books. A qualified member of our team will visit the client's home to assist with home environment assessment, preparation and materials set up. The goal will be to enable the child to become more independent and engaged. On the first visit, the consultant will assess the family needs and get approval to order any prescribed furniture, equipment or accessories. We will discuss design changes to realize fine and gross motor opportunities, improve practical life in the home, and present materials ideas. On the second visit, the consultant will prepare the environment with the added purchases and parents' involvement. The third visit will occur two months later, and the impact of the changes will be assessed, and the need for further changes will be contemplated and acted upon. Cost: $499 Flat fee for 3 visits.

Example: https://www.theintentionalnanny.com/services/p/style-01-nf5p8
Resource: https://www.sciencedirect.com/topics/psychology/home-environment

Library Design Consultancy

We will consult with preschools and families at-home, on how-to design a reading library that will foster a love for reading and learning. We will suggest and provide a variety of print materials, props, wall finishes, and furniture design, to create a cozy place. We will also design the layout of the area, including small chairs and tables, couches, bookshelves, magazine racks, storage cabinets, audio/visual devices, floor pillows, beanbag seating, writing desk, and nook reading lamps. We will oversee every aspect of the library design process.

Resource: https://preschool.org/set-up-preschool-reading-center/
Example: https://junipercustom.com/collections/libraries

Bespoke Library Subscription Service

We will offer to help families to assemble collections of books, magazines, periodicals, and journals for their home libraries, based on an understanding of the interests and learning objectives of family members, and an awareness of publishing categories and trends. We will develop a questionnaire that helps to surface subscriber preferences. We will offer this service on a subscription basis, and ship curated book selections on a monthly or quarterly basis. We will reduce our financial risk by only purchasing books that have been pre-agreed upon, and are within the customer's budget constraints. We will also provide extra content from and about the included authors, and publish a list of the top 100 demanded books and magazines.

Resource: https://junipercustom.com/collections/grand-gesture
Examples: https://www.thelockedlibrary.co.uk/
             https://www.bespokepost.com/subscription
             http://www.rivistas.com/school-library/

Preschool Curriculum Development Consultants

As curriculum consultants, we will consult preschool administrators how to design and improve their lesson plans. We will typically work with an entire school administration to help them design, develop, and implement an effective curriculum model for the entire institution. We will assess the effectiveness of existing curricula, identify areas for improvement, and propose innovative strategies to enhance learning outcomes. The primary purpose of any curriculum proposal will be to help children to build the skills and knowledge base they need to be successful in school and life. The challenge will be to develop an early childhood curriculum, based on a proven educational philosophy, that has the flexibility to resonate with each child's innate curiosity and interests, and varied learning styles.

Directory: https://eceexperts.com/
Source: https://www.collaborative.org/consulting/early-childhood-consulting/
Resource: https://mybrightwheel.com/blog/early-childhood-curriculum

Location-Based Curriculum Development Consultancy

We will train preschool operators on how-to develop a curriculum that is location-based, and provides a sense of place. The curriculum would then be tied to the needs of or the resources available in the local community. A good location-based curriculum would make use of nearby amenities, that can enhance the preschool experience, such as parks, libraries, community centers, nature walks, farms, botanical gardens, transportation terminals, firehouses, theaters, distribution centers, museums, art galleries, playgrounds, healthy food retailers, bakeries, and medical, religious and recreational facilities.

As an example, a nature-based curriculum would be focused on what animals and plants are doing each month or season of the year, in a specific location or area. This would include: which flowers are blooming, which trees are bearing fruit. which evergreens are producing pine cones, and consequently, adjust lessons to reflect what children can and want to investigate. There will also be lessons on how-to safely use planting and harvesting tools.

Resource: www.naeyc.org/resources/pubs/yc/jul2015/sense-of-place-human-geography
Example: www.jovial.org/community/how-to-start-a-nature-preschool

Home Daycare Business Conversion Consultants

We will consult on how-to open a home daycare. We will provide help with location finding, choosing a business entity type, submitting licensing and business forms, and how-to build-in child safety features. We will and conduct a mock virtual inspection to surface deficiencies and assist with getting final approvals to launch the daycare business. We will also present a directory of business and resource contacts, advise on emergency preparedness planning, and how-to write an operating manual with best practices. We will also recommend and help to install accounting software and management systems, and implement proposed marketing programs.

Examples:
Home Daycare Summit   www.homedaycaresummit.com/consulting
Emergent Ed   https://emergentedccc.com/products/licensed-child-care-home
Childcare Biz Help   www.childcarebizhelp.com/services/child-care-consulting/
Early Education Business Consultants   www.earlyeducationbusiness.com/

Procare Software   www.procaresoftware.com
Software features include: online registration, billing, collecting tuition, mobile payments, and the clock-in/clock-out.

Preschool Business Brokerage
We will become licensed real estate brokers with a focus exclusively on the sale and purchase of preschools in certain states. We will bring our ___ (#) years of management and ownership experience to our preschool clients. We will also remain active members of many childcare and early education associations, such as: National Association for the Education of Young Children, to stay informed about current industry trends. We will become experts in determining the value of a preschool using a number of business valuation methods.

Source: https://www.valuadder.com/blog/business-valuation-day-care/
                 https://appraisersforum.com/forums/threads/valuing-a-child-care-centre.183196/
Examples: http://www.preschoolbusinesssolutions.com/home-1
                 https://www.trademarcpreschoolrealty.com/
Resource: https://synergybb.com/for-business-owners/sell-your-daycare-preschool/

XXIX.   Incorporate WOW Design Elements

We will incorporate the following design elements to create a WOW impression, both inside and outside the preschool:
1.   Designate one room for imaginative play activities and to host parties.
2.   Use soft and calming colors to create a comfortable and playful environment.
3.   Use combinations of colors that have special meaning for a particular target audience or culture.
4.   Place a bulletin board at the entrance to every classroom, and display the daily classroom schedule, teacher profile, and an overview of the curriculum.
5.   Provide a computer terminal, in a dedicated workspace, to acquaint students with technology, on a limited basis.
6.   Mount a smart TV, with interactive capabilities, on the classroom wall to enable post video watching discussions.
7.   Avoid clutter and provide clear lines of sight for supervision purposes.
8.   Provide design flexibility with furniture on wheels, movable walls, and efficient uses of space to allow for different modes of learning.
9.   Arrange low-profile furniture to make it easy for students to access materials and teachers to supervise and interact with the students.
10.   Incorporate soundproofing strategies to minimize noise disruptions.
11.   Install large windows to maximize access to natural light sources and nature views, to reduce stress and enable focus and concentration, and realize the biophilia effect.
12.   Choose flooring and work surface materials that create safe (non-skid), comfortable and easy-to-clean surfaces.

13. Create a visually harmonious space by matching colors.
14. Address safety concerns and potential hazards by the use soft curves and arcs, and cushioned materials.
15. Create specific learning areas, such as for open reading or a mini-library area, writing tables, block playing, sensory table, and an artists' workstation.
16. Decorate based on the aesthetic and educational needs of the children, and introduce an element of fun to maintain student interest.
17. Use decorations and visuals that are durable, vibrant, inclusive and spark learning.
18. Change the décor with the seasons to capture the themes of spring, summer, autumn, and winter.
19. Match the decorations to a book or curriculum theme, and change them on a monthly basis to keep children engaged.
20. Provide adequate storage cabinets and closets for coat racks, cubbies and/or lockers.
21. Create a secure cabinet for the medical first aid kit.
22. Place a whiteboard, chalkboard, or Smart-Board on a feature wall.
23. Start a music program and make musical instruments available.
24. Install outdoor playsets that provide a safe and fun environment, such as cushioned, rubberized, flooring materials under climbing frames, slides, and swings.
25. Build a portable puppet stage, because puppet performances create a range of learning opportunities and a playful atmosphere.
26. Explore design ideas to create a comfortable, preschool reading corner, with cozy blankets, rugs, pillows, cushions and beanbags.
    Source: www.pinterest.com/pattityler/preschool-reading-corner/

Resources: www.pinterest.com/madamquierie/preschool-design/
www.behance.net/search/projects/preschool%20interior%20design?locale=en_US
Source:
https://www.childcarerenovation.com/preschool-classroom-design-principles/
https://simplifiedplaygrounds.com/blogs/blog/how-to-attract-parents-to-your-child-care-center

XXX.   Manage Operating Costs

We will pursue the following strategies to manage and reduce our operating costs:
1. Every year ask service providers to submit bids for new contract periods, in an attempt to find or negotiate better deals or customer service.
2. Look for innovative ways to get food program costs under control, such as via bulk purchases of fast-moving products (see below).
3. Setup sub-accounts and use automatic transfers to make funds available for major expense categories, such as rent, food, taxes and salaries.
4. Purchase used toys, equipment and furniture from closing businesses, and via eBay.com, Facebook Marketplace and Craigslist.
5. Offer incentives for staff members to submit suggestions to cut costs or improve productivity.

6. Assign team leader responsibilities, and provide incentives to beat the budgeted and forecasted expenses by department, on a monthly basis.
7. Engage in flexible or floating staffing by moving teachers between classrooms based on occupancy levels and curriculum requirements.
8. Offer flexible contracts of employment to reduce payroll costs during lower enrollment periods.
9. Reduce the occurrence of bad debts by instituting a formal and early process for debt collection.
10. Create systems to capture rainwater and purify gray water for landscaping purposes.
11. Outsource admin functions to expert professionals, if significant money can be saved, or the time requirements to not require full-time employees.
12. Determine if discounts, up to 5%, are given for early or automatic payments on invoices.
13. Offer rewards for employees who identify inefficiencies or "whistle blow" on wasteful or inefficient operations.
14. Sell or rent unused space or equipment.
15. Reduce the need for expensive debt financing, by increasing the speed of invoice processing and payments processing.
16. Enable certain admin functions to be performed remotely to reduce space rental expenses.

Resource: https://www.bill.com/blog/reducing-operating-costs-and-expenses

Get Food Program Costs Under Control

Our objective will be to serve tasty, nutritious meals, at a cost savings, using the following tactics:

1. Compare the cost savings of store and generic brands to national brands.
2. Turn leftovers into next day soups.
3. Buy fast moving food items in bulk packaged units, such as pasta and rice.
4. Limit purchases of perishables to quantities actually being consumed.
5. Buy locally grown, fresh produce, that is in season.
6. Buy cheeses in bulk because of their many applications, including Mac n cheese.
7. Purchase frozen chicken nuggets and meatballs in bulk because of their popularity, and shelf-life, if properly stored.
8. Buy staples in bulk from warehouse stores.
9. Plan menus at least a week in advance to seize buying opportunities.
10. Purchase trays of prepared foods from a caterer, and convert to individualized portions.
11. Investigate the availability of federal and state funded food programs.
12. Research efficient, ventless cooking and warming commercial kitchen equipment, to reduce the expense of code compliance.

Notes:

Ventless commercial cooking equipment does not require an overhead traditional ventilation system to be operated. The ovens are designed to carry away grease, smoke, or other cooking vapors.

Food Program Resources:

The Child and Adult Care Food Program (CACFP)   www.fns.usda.gov/cacfp

This is a federal program that provides reimbursements for nutritious meals and snacks to eligible children and adults who are enrolled for care at participating child care centers, day care homes, and adult day care centers. CACFP also provides reimbursements for meals served to children and youth participating in afterschool care programs, children residing in emergency shelters, and adults over the age of 60 or living with a disability and enrolled in day care facilities.

The National School Lunch Program   **https://www.fns.usda.gov/nslp**
NSLP is a federally assisted meal program operating in public and nonprofit private schools and residential child care institutions. It provides nutritionally balanced, low-cost or free lunches to children each school day.

Family Resources   **https://familyresourcesinc.org/child-care-food-program/**
Provides meal reimbursements to enrolled licensed family child care providers who are providing nutritious, well-balanced meals to the children in their care.

Equipment:
TurboChef   **https://turbochef.com/**
TurboChef impingement ovens utilize precisely controlled top and bottom air to increase heat transfer rates, resulting in cook times that are 40–50% faster.
Directory: www.webstaurantstore.com/guide/962/ventless-commercial-cooking-equipment-buying-guide.html

Lower Insurance Premium Costs

We will take the following actions to lower our insurance risks and resulting insurance premium costs:

1. Get all company vehicles routinely inspected by a licensed mechanic.
2. Install fleet telematics or GPS tracking.
3. Keep alarm installed vehicles in a well-lit, fenced-in area to deter theft.
4. Add "no child left behind" alarm systems to vehicles that transport children.
5. Provide driver safety training programs for all vehicle operating employees.
6. Annually have professionally inspected all major systems, such as plumbing, electrical, HVAC, video surveillance, exterior lighting and roofing.
7. Prevent water damage by ensuring access to secure water shut-off values.
8. Protect the fire sprinkler system from freezing, during the cold weather, by insulating pipes.
9. Replace water heaters, near their end of their life expectancy, to prevent leaks and water damage, and purchase a more efficient model.
10. Keep drains, gutters, and roofs free of debris.
11. Invest in backup generators, water detection sensors, door alarms. and video surveillance cameras or streaming apps for added security.
12. Conduct monthly staff trainings on how to avoid regulation and licensing violations.
13. Create a mentorship program to pair new employees with experienced team members who can provide appropriate safety information and controls.

14. Maintain lower student-to-teacher ratios, than required, to reduce the occurrence of accidents.
15. Install more durable, rubberized, fall zone, surfacing materials in outdoor play areas.
16. Utilize anti-slip floor mats and runners in wet areas.
17. Get commercial playground equipment annually inspected by a certified playground inspector.
18. Regularly inspect and repair playground fencing and gates.
19. Develop safety procedures for the storage and use of hazardous substances.
20. Develop an accident reporting and investigation system that can learn from and prevent future recurrences.
21. Develop a reputation for proactively implementing safety protocols and procedures to prevent claims from occurring, in the first place.
22. Highlight insurance risk reduction measures in the policy and procedure manuals.
23. Develop disaster recovery and business continuity plans to survive a crisis, such as a cyber-crime or a windstorm.
24. Combine different coverages under a bundled policy to get a better overall rate.
25. Regularly evaluate deductibles, while knowing about the ability to pay a higher deductible amount up-front, if a claim is necessary.
26. Ask about the availability of a claims-free or low usage discount.
27. Keep good business and personal credit ratings.
28. Sign-up for the payment method that saves money, such as automatic or upfront.
29. Ask about the availability of group rates, such as through a trade association.
30. Lower deductibles, but be ready to do some self-insuring.

Source: www.grangeinsurance.com/tips/five-ways-to-lower-business-insurance-premium
https://tivly.com/reduce-business-insurance-costs
https://www.business.com/insurance/saving-tips/

XXXI.   Staff Retention Strategies

Reduce the Teacher Turnover Rate

We will use the following proven methods to increase teacher retention and mitigate the significant costs associated with burnout stress and a high turnover rate:

1. Develop monitoring and responsive corrective action programs.
2. Tie higher salaries to individual performance ratings and preschool profitability.
3. Provide more opportunities, such as weekly meetings, for teachers to collaborate with each other and an assigned mentor.
4. Give teachers the physical resources and supplies they need to be successful.
5. Give teachers the chance to realize up-skilling opportunities by participating in conferences, e-learning courses, workshops, and webinars.
6. Implement comprehensive onboarding and continuing education programs.
7. Support teachers by listening to their feedback and giving them more opportunities

to express their opinions and concerns at monthly 1-on-1 meetings with administrators.

8. Promote a positive preschool culture where both teachers and students feel safe, trusted, and respected.
9. Give teachers more control over the way in which their classrooms are managed.
10. Implement monthly team-building activities and offer opportunities for group decision-making.
11. Show appreciation for employees with consistent hours, appreciation awards and bonuses.
12. Offer scheduling flexibility, with the opportunity to work a short shift, or leave early for personal reasons.
13. Provide job enrichment opportunities by exposing staffers to extra 'free time' tasks, such as records organizing, student assessments, teacher mentoring, marketing support, bookkeeping and classroom observations.
14. Use recruiting tools and job descriptions to hire the right employees and manage expectations.
15. Monitor the salaries offered by competitors and remain competitive.
16. Stay abreast of industry trends.
17. Clearly define a career path and the milestones to be achieved.
18. Assign special projects to teachers to show confidence and provide the opportunity to learn new skills.
19. Conduct retention surveys and exit interviews to uncover the basis for decisions.
20. Offer a 'guaranteed' number or work hours.
21. Offer staff tuition discounts to their family members.
22. Give staff the option to take extra paid days off instead of other types of rewards for excellent performance.
23. Give recognition awards, such as certificates or trophies, and gift vouchers, for employee of the month and year.
24. Start a mentoring program that is perceived as being positive and supportive.
25. Develop a written training agreement that allows a percent of training costs to be reclaimed, based on when the employee leaves.

Enhance the Teaching Credentials of Staff Members

We will encourage all full-time employees to earn an associate and bachelor's degree in 'Early Childhood Education' for free, at participating online schools, with flexible schedules. All tuition, fees and books will be covered. This program will give our preschool teachers the ability to continue their education, grow their career opportunities, and become aware of new teaching methods, while simultaneously improving the quality of education for students.

Employees will be required to stay with the company for at least __ (18?) months after earning their degree. The schools will be accredited by the National Association for the Education of Young Children. Examples of participating schools include:

Northampton Community College	Ashton University
Walden University	Rasmussen College

Directory: www.bestcolleges.com/education/bachelors/early-childhood-education/
https://regportal.flchild.com/degreedatabase

Example: https://careers.brighthorizons.com/us/en/horizons-teacher-degree
Source: www.insidehighered.com/news/2018/08/15/free-college-tuition-day-care-
             center-workers-strings-attached

Develop Internal Teacher Training Programs

We will advise our teachers that training should be a continuous process, and assessments will be regularly conducted to appraise material retention and application. Additionally, annual reviews will consider the effects of training programs on teacher performance ratings.

The training programs will address the following issues and challenges:

1. Teachers take turns sharing the insights they have gained from experiences in the preschool.
2. Help teachers to develop an understanding of the preschool core values, culture, educational philosophy, and mission and vision statements, so they can practice and teach them to new recruits.
3. Teach how to maintain open lines of communication with parents to maximize the value of the content in student progress reports.
4. Make everyone aware of the new enhanced cleaning practices and procedures.
5. Provide an explanation of the preschool's education and teaching philosophies, and the source materials to be used.
6. Keep teachers posted as to the tasks, issues, needs and challenges facing the preschool.
7. Train teachers on the 'best practice', teaching methods that will improve student test scores and social development skills.
7. Train teachers on how-to promote, administer and benefit from the referral programs.
8. Share the strategy for handling complaints and conveying solutions to the parents.
9. Develop a generic sales training class to provide tour givers with baseline selling skills.
10. Develop a pool of more Director qualified employees.
11. Train teachers to improve indoor and outdoor child safety.
12. Inform teachers how to recognize and report signs of child abuse.

Source: https://preschoolinspirations.com/5-online-trainings-for-preschool-teachers/
Resource: www.childcaresuccess.com/how-to-close-tours-in-your-child-care-business/
             www.mcfattertechnicalcollege.edu/early-childhood-education/

Know the Priorities of Millennial Teachers

To maximize the return on investment in our millennial teachers, we will need to know more about their motivations and hot button issues. Research indicates that millennial teachers have the following generalized priorities and interests:

1. Have a concern with social matters and protecting the environment.
2. Like to work to make change happen and realize bigger good causes.
3. Appreciate a thank you for doing good work.
4. Welcome leadership position opportunities
5. Are more plugged into and familiar with technology and current trends.
6. Value collaborative team roles and investments in their career development.
7. Like to have their opinions asked for and respected.
8. Like employee and parent referral programs that provide real incentives.

9. Respond to annual surveys that give them a voice and ask for improvement suggestions.
10. Show more understanding and empathy for students.
11. Have a greater interest in workplace diversity to foster creativity and innovation.
12. Seek a better work/life balance and want to be lifelong learners.
13. Want to be compensated based on quality-of-work or results, and not years of service.

Source: https://content.acsa.org/10-ways-to-encourage-and-engage-millennial-educators/
Resource: www.focuswise.com/blog/the-millennial-mindset-8-lessons-we-can-all-learn

Conduct Teacher Evaluations and Appraisal Reviews
We will ask the following questions to assess the impact of staff training investments:
1. What training programs have you participated in?
2. What new skills have you acquired?
3. What difference has the training made to your performance?
4. What other career development needs should be addressed?
5. What are the things that you want to learn more about?
6. How can the training programs be improved?
7. What would you suggest doing to improve the preschool's growth prospects?

XXXII.   Conduct Competitor Analysis

Develop a List of Competitive Advantages
During the parent tours we will present a list of our competitive advantages, and not only include them in our sales presentative folder, and other marketing materials, but also discuss them, in detail, with the parents. We will decide which of the following competitive advantages to pursue in greater detail, and which to delete from the list:
Resource:
www.childcaremarketing.com/using-competitive-advantage-attract-parents-daycare/

1. **Flexible Customized Student Scheduling**
    The objective is to accommodate the schedules of working parents. The day is divided into half-day blocks, and students can enroll in half-day or full-day or extended day and/or after-school programs. Parents can also decide the number of days they want their child to attend the preschool. Families will also be able to enroll their children at any time of the year.
    Example: www.fusionacademy.com/about/customized-options-academic-flexibility/

2. **Ala Carte Care Services**
    We will offer year-round flexible daycare options, like part time daycare and drop in daycare. Combinations of wrap-around care services will be available to meet the specific needs of families.

Example: www.lapetite.com/educational-programs/drop-in-care/
             https://alacartelearning.com/

3.   **Teacher Formal Education Requirements/Accreditations**
     Teachers have an Early-Childhood Development Associates Degree or a four-year
     College Bachelor's Degree in a related-field. Teachers have earned NAEYC
     Accreditation, the mark of quality and excellence for early childhood education.
     The program is also 4 Star Parent Aware rated.
     Resource: https://www.naeyc.org/events/trainings-webinars
     Source: Cognia   https://www.cognia.org

4.   **Highly Qualified and Experienced Teachers**
     All of our teachers are required to have at least an Associate's Degree, and ___ (#)
     years work experience in a childcare setting. Our preschool teachers start out as
     childcare workers or teacher assistants.
     Resource: https://www.truity.com/career-profile/preschool-teacher

5.   **Teacher On-site or Online Training Programs**
     We schedule ___ (5?) days of all-hands, team-based, or online training every year
     to keep teacher skills updated and reinforce our core values, mission statement and
     culture.
     Resource:
     https://preschoolinspirations.com/5-online-trainings-for-preschool-teachers/

6.   **In-house Child Behavioral Coach Certifications**
     We have produced the video tutorials and proprietary apps to offer educators access
     to a variety of resources and tools to help promote positive skills development and
     realize new learning opportunities in the classroom.

7.   **Encourage Parent Support and Participation**
     Parents are always welcome in our classrooms, and our early-childhood specialists
     are open to meeting outside of class to help answer parent questions or respond to
     issues. We will also develop a list of parent participation projects for which they can
     earn tuition credits.

8.   **Hold Parent Learning Events**
     Seminar speakers and parent social events are provided throughout the school year,
     to further face-to-face interactions, and parenting skills development, at no additional
     cost, to only actively enrolled student parents.
     Resource: www.edutopia.org/article/meaningful-parent-events/

9.   **Creatively Blended Teaching Philosophies**
     We will use our own uniquely developed creative or blended curriculum model, as the
     basis of our lessons and classroom designs. It will combine the best practices of several
     education philosophies, including Montessori, STEM, HighScope, Reggio Emilia,
     Waldorf, Co-ops, Religious, and Bank Street. The special features of the merged

curriculums will provide hands-on experiences for children to enrich the learning experience and reach the stated learning goals for each lesson. Realizing differentiated instruction will be an important part of this personalized learning experience. We will also combine instructor-led brick-and-mortar classroom training and online learning activities.

Resources: www.edutopia.org/article/implementing-blended-learning-pre-k-students/
www.beginlearning.com/parent-resources/blended-learning/
https://brighterly.com/blog/pre-school-philosophy/

10. **Child Performance Metrics: Ongoing Learning Monitoring**

Student learning assessments are continually tracked and reported through teacher observation notes on academic knowledge, social skills and speaking ability, work-sample portfolios, group interaction assessments, and a developmental continuum student packet. We will develop a standardized set of child progress merits, and make their presentation a focus of our parent-teacher meetings. Their purpose will be to show areas where, the parents can work with the child at home to improve performance and guide curriculum choices.

Resource: https://nap.nationalacademies.org/read/18845/chapter/8#46
www.procaresoftware.com/blog/preschool-assessment-what-to-expect/

11. **Participation as Sponsors of Community Events**

We will specialize in the offering of in-kind sponsorships, which refers to the providing of goods or services, such as educational materials, instead of financial support. These events include Fall/Harvest Parties, Grandparent's Day, Arts and Crafts Fairs, Christmas Programs, Valentine's Day, Easter-Egg Hunts, Golf Invitationals, Music Programs, Sports Tournaments, and Graduations.

Example: https://www.preschooladvantage.org/become-an-event-sponsor/

12. **Low Teacher to Student Ratios**

Student–teacher ratio or student–faculty ratio is the number of students who attend a school divided by the number of teachers in the institution. For example, a student–teacher ratio of 10:1 indicates that there are 10 students for every one teacher. Research indicates that at the age of 3, children can thrive in classrooms of up to 10 students, which is the ratio we will maintain.

Resource:
www.mychildcareacademy.com/the-benefits-of-low-student-to-teacher-ratios-in-childcare/

13. **Live Streaming Video**

We will increase transparency and keep families connected, with the safest and highest-quality streaming video camera system available. This technology allows families to feel informed, engaged, and connected with their children throughout the day.

Resource:

Watch Me Grow   https://watchmegrow.com

It helps childcare centers increase transparency and keep families connected, with high-quality streaming video camera systems.

Directory: https://watchmegrow.com/parents/find-school

Illumine   https://illumine.app/live-streaming/
Illumine lets users monitor and control camera access efficiently, while also letting users to charge parents for the live streaming feature, if you wish to.

14. **Digital Parent Communication Apps**
These apps will enable teachers take photos of the children throughout the day and transmit them to parents.
Example: www.pathwayslearningacademy.com/our-schools/parent-app/
Resources: www.lifecubby.me
                www.kidreports.com
                www.tadpoles.com
SproutAbout   https://play.google.com/store/apps/details/SproutAbout?id=com.
                learningcaregroup.sproutabout&hl=en_SG
This is an all-in-one, custom-built early childhood education app that was designed to take family communication to the next level.

15. **Greater Integration of Technology and Digital Systems**
We will continue to integrate technology, as a way to enhance the learning experience for the children, and streamline administrative tasks for the staff. These will include: smartphones, laptops, smart TVs, tablets, interactive whiteboards, digital storytelling, interactive lesson platforms, and virtual reality and augmented reality systems.
We will provide opportunities for children to begin to explore and feel comfortable using touchscreens or "traditional" mouse and keyboard computers, to use Websites or look up answers with a search engine. We will also capture digital photos of children-created block buildings or artwork, and videotape dramatic play to replay for children. We will train our teachers to have and share their greater degree of digital literacy. They will also use and hand-out tablets with touch-screen features, to provide students with access to digital learning resources. Lesson plans will also be video-recorded and represented on wall-mounted Smart TVs. We will also use smart boards with touch screen interactive whiteboards.
Source:
https://www.hatchearlylearning.com/
https://elearningindustry.com/using-technology-in-the-classroom-benefits-and-top-tips

16. **Local Business and Church Partnerships**
We have formed partnerships with local businesses and churches to offer on-site daycare and preschool services, as a convenient employee benefit. We have been able to put the saved rental overhead expenses back into the quality of the learning experiences delivered to the children.
Resource:
Encourage Preschools   www.encouragepreschools.net/church-partnership-models/
They partner with churches across the U.S. to provide the support they need for launching a thriving preschool from their existing venue.

17. **Customized Curriculum Offerings**

We developed a proprietary digital lesson planning tool to empower our educators to efficiently generate customized curriculum, for each child, based on performance metrics. Our objective is to deliver personalized learning experiences.
Resource:
Assessment Technology, Inc.   https://www.ati-online.com/
A provider of integrated assessment, curriculum, and reporting services.

18.   **Focus on Children's Health and Wellness**
The preschool has been certified as eco-healthy, and we have developed programs that help children manage stress better and prevent obesity. They will also learn about nutrition and the benefits of exercise, yoga and meditation. We will train the staff in CPR, first aid and Child Abuse Awareness and Prevention.
Resource: https://healthpoweredkids.org/
Examples:
www.prekprintablefun.com/blog/20-preschool-activities-that-promote-good-health
Source: www.peacehealth.org/healthy-you/teaching-kids-stay-healthy

19.   **Focus on an Arts Program for Children**
We will encourage the children to express their ideas and feelings through their art. Active experiences in art will be designed to develop visual, spatial and manipulative skills. We will teach the following types of the visual arts: painting, clay modelling, sculpture, collage making, weaving, construction, photography, wearable art, and printing. We will take the Japanese approach, and encourage the children to mix their paint colors on the paper to create new colors.
Resource: www.deepspacesparkle.com/top-eight-tips-for-teaching-art-to-children/
https://theeducationhub.org.nz/an-introduction-to-the-visual-arts-in-early-childhood-education/

20.   **Build Children's Creative Intelligence**
We will offer hope and a pathway to those who fear the onslaught of Artificial Intelligence and the loss of many jobs in the marketplace. We will develop a learning environment that nurtures children's creative intelligence, by allowing them to think-outside-the-box, to solve problems. We will foster the development of creative thinking, which is the act of diverging one's thinking to explore many different problem-solving options. We will provide open-ended questions that encourage students to think outside-the-box and to collaborate with each other to creatively solve problems. We will coach families, in workshops, how to provide positive family support for creative thinking at-home. We will create design art exhibitions that showcase child creations and present awards to the top three creative thinkers.
Resource:
https://everydayspeech.com/sel-implementation/a-practical-guide-to-teaching-creative-problem-solving-in-elementary-education/

21.   **Formal Kindergarten Readiness Program**
A top priority will be to ready children for a successful transition to kindergarten by focusing on the following area of child development:

Expressive language skills	Developing curiosity
Problem solving	Physical motor skills
Social and emotional development	Early academic skills
Basic learning skills	Sense of independence
Self-control	Artistic Expression

Resource: www.firstthingsfirst.org/resources/kindergarten-readiness/
https://childdevelopment.com.au/areas-of-concern/kindergarten-readiness/

22.   **30-Day Family Satisfaction Guarantee**
If at any time during the first 30 days of enrollment, the parent is unhappy with
the preschool, and wishes to withdraw their child, we will refund the tuition money,
with no limitations.

23.   **Safe, Fully-Equipped Playground**
We will install outdoor playground structures that are designed for children. It will
create a safe and fun play environment, that will promote physical activity, imagination
and social skills development. We will thoroughly investigate the building of shaded
or covered areas, and the use of safer surfacing materials, such as rubber outdoor mats
and shredded rubber. Additionally, all posts will be wrapped with foam padding, and
gates will have childproof safety latches.
Resource:
www.playgroundequipment.com/products/commercial-playgrounds/play-systems/
Source: https://coloradokidspeds.com/Playground-Safety-1
            https://pathways.org/outdoor-play-safety-tips/
https://childcare.extension.org/basic-tips-to-keep-children-in-child-care-safe-outdoors/

24.   **Outdoor Classroom Projects**
We will design an engaging outdoor learning environment around a garden or
greenhouse. In the outdoor classroom, children will connect to the natural world and
learn from what nature has to teach us. There will be various planting, gardening,
weeding, fertilizing, landscaping, and harvesting projects. The goal of the
exposure to the natural environment will be to enhance children's creativity and
imagination, as they play and explore. It will also improve their social skills and
teamwork as they interact with other children and wildlife.
Source: https://www.outdoorclassroomproject.org/
            https://mybrightwheel.com/blog/outdoor-classroom
Resource:
www.daycarestudio.net/home/howtomakeyourchildcarebusinessstandout

25.   **Nutritious Hot Lunch, Breakfast and Snacks**
Balanced lunches will include an entree, sides of organic fruit and veggies, as well as
organic milk. We will provide children with two nutritious, healthy snacks at no extra
cost.
Resources: https://nutritioninbloom.com/blog/2018/preschool-lunch-ideas-jlxaz
            https://funcheaporfree.com/healthy-snacks-for-kids/

26. **In-house Commercial Kitchen**
   All meals are cooked in-house under 'Child and Adult Care Food Program' guidelines. This kitchen will give us complete control over the following factors: quality and freshness of organic ingredients, daily menu choices, recipes and ingredients used, the timeliness of the delivery, food presentation, personalization options, etc. It may also allow us to save on the costs of preparing these meals, versus using the services of an outside catering company
   Resources:
   https://training.drdaycare.com/product/running-a-kitchen-at-a-child-care-center/
   https://www.tiktok.com/discover/commercial-kitchen-for-daycare

27. **State-of-the-Art Security System**
   We will implement advanced security measures to safeguard students, with controlled entry systems, surveillance cameras and enforced visitor policies. We will develop the following systems and procedures, and install digital systems to improve the security of the facility and students:
   - Motion-detected video surveillance cameras
   - Database of approved and unauthorized visitors, using facial recognition software.
   - Practice digitally updated and distributed emergency preparedness plans.
   - Electronic door locks and security gates that advise when accessed.
   - Digital systems, including fingerprint scanner, keycard, or coded entry.
   - Audible alarms, text or email notifications, or mobile apps to give parents real-time updates on emergency situations.
   - Enforce strict pick-up and drop-off procedures with a password-protected app.
   - Require the wearing of official staff identification badges.
   - Conduct regular risk assessment reviews by qualified law enforcement professionals.

   Resource: https://mybrightwheel.com/blog/daycare-security
   Examples: https://www.green-roots.com/why-choose-us/security/
                      https://www.cedargablespreschool.com/safety

28. **Non-toxic Use of Cleaning Materials**
   We will primarily use all-natural cleaning products that use lemon juice, castile soap, hydrogen peroxide, pine essential oils, white vinegar, borax, and baking soda, as key ingredients. The white vinegar will be used to clean surfaces, remove stains and deodorize, while baking soda will be used as a mild abrasive cleaner.

   Resource: https://daycarecleaningservices.com/non-toxic-cleaning-chemicals-for-use-in-daycare-centers/

29. **Convenient Location Access**
   Our preschool will be conveniently located for parents, such as near residential neighborhoods or major employment centers. We will also consider the commuting patterns and transportation options in the area. Our location will have adequate parking spaces, and convenient and safe drop-off and pick-up areas. It will also have

a good proximity to parks, playgrounds, and other amenities that can enhance the children's developmental and learning experiences.

Source: https://childcaredaily.org/location-matters-unveiling-the-secrets-of-finding-the-ideal-spot-for-your-childcare-business/

30. **On-site After-School Enrichment Programs**
Our students will be able to attend after-school enrichment programs without having to be transported to another location, Classes will be available in music, art, piano, yoga, dance, technology, coding, Lego building, robotics, and cooking. We will also provide transportation services for students wanting to attend from other local preschools. We will promote these programs by offering the booking of a free virtual tour or on-site trial class.
Example: https://makerkids.com/book-a-trial-class/
Source: https://www.rightatschool.com/
Examples: www.kindercare.com/programs-curriculum/additional-programs/
                     before-after-school-programs
               https://makerkids.com/after-school-programs/
               www.primroseschools.com/education/before-after-school
               https://www.hialeahgardensafterschool.com/

31. **Activities are All-Inclusive**
Children with special needs will take part in the general education curriculum, based on their ages and grades. They are not put into a separate classroom, but rather the curriculum and the room are adapted to meet children's needs. Assistant teachers will focus on children who need personalized support in key developmental areas. We will create an environment in which everyone feels safe, welcome, respected, comfortable and cared for.
Source: https://mybrightwheel.com/blog/inclusive-classroom
www.teachearlyyears.com/a-unique-child/view/inclusion-in-early-years-settings

32. **Weekly Student Progress Reports**
We will email a weekly student progress report to provide parents with valuable insights into their child's progress, in key developmental areas, such as social-emotional, language, cognitive, physical skills and work habits. We will also include any goals and next steps, and provide families with any resources or suggestions to support their child. We will welcome return emails from parents wanting to work together to solve a problem.
Resources:
https://mybrightwheel.com/blog/preschool-progress-report
www.splashlearn.com/blog/giving-the-right-report-card-comments-free-samples/

33. **Quarterly Child Assessments**
Each child will be assessed three times per year to ensure that their developmental progress is on track. The assessments will be immediately followed by parent/teacher conferences. At these conferences, parents will be welcomed to express their concerns, and teachers may suggest additional programs and home support activities.

Example: https://www.parklandchildrensacademy.com/

34.   **State Certified Preschool Curriculum**
        We will use the state's Department of Education Standards for all our classes. The standards and benchmarks will reflect the knowledge and skills that a child on a developmental progression, should know and be able to do at the end of an age-related timeframe.
        Resource: https://flbt5.floridaearlylearning.com/

35.   **Privately Owned and Operated by a Local Family**
        Our preschool will be owned and operated by a local family, who is readily available to discuss solutions to parent's concerns.

36.   **Meal Plan Options**
        Parents will be given the option of purchasing meals from our catering company or supplying lunch from home themselves. All the children will receive complimentary mid-morning and afternoon snacks, and pizza on Fridays. We will provide well-balanced, age-appropriate snacks, prepared based on the child's dietary requirements and allergies. All food served will be organic and peanut free.
        Example: https://risetothetoppreschool.com/our-programs/

37.   **Large Indoor Play Area Can Be Rented for Family Events**
        We will verify that our preschool location is properly zoned for an indoor playground or entertainment facility, and obtain the required health and safety, occupancy and fire safety permits. We will first market this family play area to enrolled families and then to nearby preschools and homeschoolers. The featured toddler zone will have smaller slides, soft play toys, and seating around the perimeter for parents and small parties.
        Resource: https://www.roller.software/blog/open-indoor-playground
        Example: https://kidclubhouse.com/ways-to-play/

38.   **Scheduling Convenience for Parents**
        We do not shut-down for school vacations or government holidays, but rather provide continuous child care services, with no calendar gaps. On traditional school close days, weeks and months, we will transition to a traditional daycare center.

39.   **Detailed Emergency Plan of Action**
        We have contingency plans and practice drills for every possible occurrence, including natural disasters, and an operations manual that describes how to handle all possible scenarios.
        Source: www.aus.com/security-resources/be-prepared-7-components-emergency-plan
              www.childcareaware.org/our-issues/crisis-and-disaster-resources/child-care-emergency-preparedness/

40.   **Year-Round Extended Care Program**
        There are no gaps in the schedule, for holidays or summer vacation, which means that both the parent and children are given more consistent support. This program will

be offered to those students enrolled in our 2, 3 or, pre-k full-day programs and who require extended daycare 12 months a year between the hours of 7am-6pm.
Example: www.getreadysetgrow.com/year-round-extended-care-program/

41.   Multiple Payment Options

We will enable families to use the form of automated payment they prefer; credit card or direct deposit from their checking account. We will offer a Tuition and Fee Installment Plan (TIP), which is an alternative to the single payment of fees due at the beginning of each semester. A nonrefundable service fee will be charged to students for the Tuition and Fee Installment Plan.

Software Resource: https://www.tuitionexpress.com/
                      https://paysimple.com/blog/daycare-payments/

42.   Offer Multiple Field Trip Options

These field trips will help kids learn in a hands-on way. They will see how their lessons in the classroom translate to the real world. We will prepare the following list of field trip options, and give parents a form on which they can prioritize their choices for desired trips, and indicate if they want to be a chaperone:

Restaurant/Café	Fitness Center
Bakery	Fire Station
Supermarket	Home Improvement Store
Library	Nursing Home
Park	Animal Shelter
Farmers Market	Beach
Art Gallery	Children's Museum
Hospital	Auto Dealership
Apple Orchard	Aquarium
Children's Theater	Farm
Petting Zoo	Skating Rink
Bowling Alley	Planetarium
Airfield	

Resource: https://www.pre-kpages.com/field-trips/

43.   Gifted Student Program

We will offer gifted education programs that focus on enrichment, higher-level instruction, academic acceleration, faster-paced curriculums and advanced materials. We will help parents to stay informed about their child's educational experience, so they can wisely advocate for appropriately challenging options. We will also offer gifted afterschool enrichment programs, and gifted weekend and summer programs. We will differentiate our core curriculum for gifted learners in the following ways:

- Place a focus on creative and critical thinking
- Provide exercises that require more complex problem solving
- Facilitate more collaborative teamwork and group interactions
- Stretch to higher order thinking processes
- Offer variable levels of pacing

- Allow for debriefing of the process
- Ask more open-ended questions
- Allow for the making of more choices

Resources:
https://k8school.com/how-to-engage-gifted-students-in-the-classroom/
www.davidsongifted.org/prospective-families/gifted-education-and-support-options/
Example:
The Gifted Child Society   https://www.gifted.org/
An educational 501(c)(3) nonprofit organization dedicated to providing tailored
enrichment programs and experiences for gifted children in preschool through high school.

44.   Responsive Transportation Services
We will leverage our best practices, technologies and processes to deliver quality
transportation solutions by licensed, background checked, trained drivers. We will
also provide afterschool transportation services to extracurricular activities or other
appointments, at local schools and businesses. We will use the 'Child Checkmate
System' which ensures that every child has disembarked form the vehicle. We will
only release children to individuals who have been authorized in writing by their
parent/guardian.
Source: https://childcheckmate.com/
Examples: www.lsapreschool.com/2-lsapreschool/10-transportation-services
Resources:
https://www.homepreschl.com/ridesharing
https://firststudentinc.com/our-services/full-service/early-childhood-services/

45.   Consistent Safety Record
To achieve a consistent safety record, we will restrict access to dangerous supplies,
implement regular handwashing protocols, daily sanitize all toys and surfaces,
practice emergency plans, maintain an unobstructed view of students, make use of
corner protectors and cushions, install non-skid flooring materials, and practice
regular floor cleanup procedures.
Resource:
www.rasmussen.edu/degrees/education/blog/preschool-classroom-safety/

46.   Daily Classroom Cleaning Checklist
We will employ strict hygiene practices to minimize the spread of germs. Our facilities
Will undergo regular safety inspections to help ensure that the children are safe. We will
develop a daily cleaning and sanitizing checklist, with assigned responsibilities, to
accomplish the following objectives:
        Run a high-quality childcare program
        Create a healthy learning environment
        Establish a consistent cleaning routine
        Minimize exposure to toxins and germs
        Easily pass state inspections.
Resource: https://mybrightwheel.com/blog/daycare-cleaning-checklist

47. **Handicap Accessibility**
We will adhere to the Americans with Disabilities Act ("ADA"), which is a federal civil rights law that Congress passed in 1990 and amended in 2008. Specifically, the ADA says that child care centers, preschools and family child care providers cannot discriminate against individuals with disabilities. We will remove all physical barriers in existing program facilities.
Resource:
https://childcare.gov/consumer-education/services-for-children-with-disabilities
www.childcarelaw.org/content/know-the-law-about-the-americans-with-disabilities-act/

48. **Décor Mentally Stimulating**
We will use the following design elements to create a visually stimulating environment for our students: contrasting colors, textures, shapes and patterns. We will incorporate interactive elements, such as sensory tables, art stations, and play areas. We will choose décor that arouses curiosity, without creating overwhelming visual clutter. We will install a bulletin board on which to display the children's artworks. We will also hang maps, hero portraits, charts and diagrams that reinforce curriculum content and lesson plans. We will also install one colorful accent wall to bring a captivating focal point of interest to the room.
Source: www.edutopia.org/article/dos-and-donts-classroom-decorations/
Resource:
www.olliandlime.com/blogs/news/5-ways-to-create-a-visually-stimulating-nursery
Examples:
www.pinterest.com/pin/mindstimulating-classroom-designs--706502260263657423/

49. **Competitive Pricing**
We will semi-annually research the pricing strategies of local preschools, while considering location and the quality and scope of care and lesson plans, to arrive at a competitive pricing strategy. We will also find ways to lower our operating costs to improve profitability without the need to raise prices.
Source:
https://tuiopay.com/blog/what-are-good-daycare-prices-that-keep-me-competitive/

50. **Semi-Annual Parent Feedback Surveys**
We will develop a childcare parent survey to gather feedback, suggestions, and valuable insights from parents to improve the quality of our child development program. The goals of these parent surveys will be to increase family engagement, evaluate programs and curriculum, collect improvement suggestions, and understand the level of parent satisfaction. We will ask for performance ratings in the following categories:

Admin Responsiveness	Participation Welcomeness
Parent Handbook Policies	Hours of Operation
Management Friendliness	Child Safety
Classroom Cleanliness	Education Quality
Curriculum Focus	Parent Communications

Child Progress Reports   Value Received

Examples: https://www.jotform.com/form-templates/preschool-parent-survey-form
https://mybrightwheel.com/blog/child-care-survey-for-parents
http://www.careformeclc.org/parent-survey.html

51.   Mastered the Art of Making Learning Fun
We will use the following tactics to make learning fun: physical activities, sing-alongs, grocery shopping role play, Lego model building, matching card games, photo-embossed jigsaw games, read picture books, watch learning cartoon videos, flashcard matching races, clay molding, toy phone playing, crafting and drawing activities, act-out flashcard stories, use child names, hands-on interactions, nature object collecting, collage making, playing homemade instruments, dynamic play areas, dancing, interactive storytelling, colored number hunts, healthy snack making, and field trips.
Resources: https://funlearningforkids.com/
https://abcgreatbeginnings.com/10-creative-and-fun-learning-activities-for-preschoolers/
Source: www.makinglearningfun.com/

52.   Dramatic Play Areas
These are places for hands-on learning. It will initially have a child kitchen, restaurant area and cookie shop bakery. The focus of the dramatic play area is a kitchen, where preschoolers can engage in home living and cooking pretend play. Additional dramatic play areas will include:

Farmers Market	Construction Site
Fire Station	Tea Party
Lemonade Stand	Donut Shop
Post Office	Gourmet Kitchen

Source:
www.amazon.com/Wood-Preschool-Kitchen-Furniture/
www.communityplaythings.com/products/play/dramatic-play/play-kitchen
Examples: https://playtolearnpreschool.us/dramatic-play-kitchen/
https://playtolearnpreschool.us/category/dramatic-play/

53.   Align Preschool Curriculum with Primary Grade Requirements
Our preschool teachers and family liaisons collaborate to align our curriculum, teacher training, and family supports, between preschool and the primary grades, for greater social-emotional development and continuum of learning. This will provide a more rewarding and smooth transition to the elementary grades. We will also move away from an emphasis on free play and spend more time on an exposure to science, literacy and math content instruction.
Resource: www.frogstreet.com/blogs/enhancing-early-learning-outcomes-through-alignment-practices/
Source: www.newamerica.org/education-policy/edcentral/new-study-highlights-the-need-for-better-alignment-between-pre-k-and-kindergarten/

54.   A Focus on Turning Children into Lifelong Learners

We will encourage students to be lifelong learners in the following ways:

a.   Encourage students to welcome challenges and view failures as opportunities to learn.
b.   Promote curiosity and inquisitiveness, by teaching that there are no stupid questions.
c.   Integrate technology and digital literacy in various programs.
d.   Listen and respond to the questions posed by children.
e.   Nurture and support the development of their interests and passions.
f.   Incorporate reading into daily routines to expand perspectives.
g.   Emphasize the importance of learning to be able to engage in more activities.
h.   Reward the learning of new skill sets and the solving of problems.
i.   Use play to develop communication, comprehension and social skills.

Resources:
https://newsinhealth.nih.gov/2016/08/help-young-kids-become-lifelong-learners
www.tutordoctor.co.uk/blog/2021/october/how-to-inspire-your-children-to-become-life-long/

55.   Teach Children the Importance of Social Responsibility

We teach children the importance of social responsibility in the following ways:

a.   Organizing drives to donate toys, games, and clothing.
b.   Planting of organic produce in gardens or flower pots.
c.   Expressing of gratitude by the writing of thank you notes.
d.   Participating in neighborhood and waterway cleanup projects.
e.   Assembling of care packages for the homeless and nursing home residents.
f.   Organizing community food drives for local food banks.
g.   Helping with chores or the caring of a pet, to experience the thrill of being helpful.
h.   Practicing acts of kindness to experience the intrinsic rewards of such actions.
i.   Teaching about the impact of making bad choices for the environment.

56.   Achieved Certification for Eco-friendliness and Sustainability

We will follow all the state guidelines and programs for a safe and environmentally friendly preschool. The program ensures that schools are as healthy as possible, for both the children and the environment. This includes practices such as buying organic and locally sourced food, using non-toxic cleaning products, recycling products, not using disposable plates and utensils, planting a school garden, collecting rainwater, re-using water bottles, and reducing energy consumption.

Source: https://overlookpreschool.com/eco-friendly/
             https://www.weareteachers.com/green-school-tips/

57.   Formed Alumni Association

We formed an alumni association of past students for the following reasons:

a.   To get alumni to attend open house events, and speak about the positive impact of their preschool experiences and share success stories.
b.   To help distribute marketing materials and participate in fundraisers.

c. To establish a network of possible connections for future graduates.
d. To obtain improvement suggestions from alumni.
e. To build a directory containing alumni profiles.
f. To obtain advertising fees from alumni formed businesses that want to market their services in the annually published alumni directory.

Example: https://fthcs.org/alumni/association/

58. **Implemented a Universal Design for Learning Environment**
The flexible learning environment has been designed to remove the barriers to learning and meet the needs of all students, regardless of their ability, dual language needs, disability, age, or size. The objective will be to support all learners, by recognizing each child's distinct culture, interests, needs, and strengths, and then using that knowledge to shape the curriculum, create multi-sensory lessons, and determine the instruction delivery methods.

Resource: https://mybrightwheel.com/blog/universal-design-for-learning

59. **On-site Commercial-Grade Kitchen**
In our commercial-grade kitchen, meals are prepared on-site by a trained cook. We follow the USDA guidelines in preparing meals and snacks, and will secure a valid food service license. We will meet or exceed all food safety requirements and food code regulations, and consistently maintain required sanitary and cold storage conditions. This kitchen will also permit our preschool business to not only provide catering services to families who rent our makerspace or playrooms for parties, but to also offer afterschool cooking classes.

Directory: https://www.afdo.org/resources/permit-and-license-laws-and-guidance/
Source:
www.publichealthlawcenter.org/datapages/food-safety-standards-child-care-settings

60. **Tuition Support for Qualifying Families**
We will help families to look for programs they are eligible for, and obtain tuition support from the following sources:
- Claim child care federal tax credits
    Resource: www.irs.gov/credits-deductions/individuals/child-and-dependent-care-credit-information
- State tax credits
    Directory: www.taxcreditsforworkersandfamilies.org/state-tax-credits/
- County Education Funding Programs
    Example: https://wildroots.com/rcoe-subsidized-funding/
- Child care subsidy programs through state and local agencies
    Directory: www.childcareaware.org/resources/map/
- Employer-provided childcare subsidies
    Resource: www.trinet.com/insights/top-childcare-benefits-to-offer-your-employees
- Programs for military and federal families
    Resource: https://childcare.gov/consumer-education/military-child-care-financial-assistance

www.childcareaware.org/families/military-child-care-
assistance-programs/

Example: www.discoverchampions.com/landing-pages/childcare-tuition-support

61.   Other Tuition Discounts for Qualifying Families
Refer-a-Friend Reward:
When friends enroll full-time, presently enrolled families can be eligible for a
tuition credit.
Sibling Discounts:
If families enroll more than one child with us, they will be offered a tuition credit.
Employee Discounts:
Employees may be eligible for other discounts or tuition credits.
Parent Earned Discounts:
Parents can earn discounts for actively participating in fundraisers, assisting with
field trips, sharing personal experiences in the classroom, performing community
outreach services, and becoming a member of the parent teach association.

62.   Offer Student Scholarships
We will provide partial student scholarships, of more than __ (?) dollars each year, to
better support qualifying families in our community. We also provide assistance to
students and teachers who want to qualify for nationally awarded scholarships.
Directory: www.earlychildhoodeducationzone.com/early-education-scholarships/
Example: https://amshq.org/Educators/Montessori-Careers/About-AMS-TEP/
                 Teacher-Education-Scholarships

63.   Work with Charities that Sponsor Children in Need
We will work with local charities that help to sponsor children from families who
cannot afford to enroll their children in early childcare development programs.
Resource: https://impactful.ninja/best-charities-for-sponsoring-a-child/
Directory: www.wheelsforwishes.org/news/21-kids-charities-to-give-to-this-year/

64.   Offer Free Trial Period
We will offer a free two-day trial period to help parents to establish a childcare
pattern and make an informed enrollment decision, and enable school administrators
to gather valuable feedback and data from interested families.
Example:
www.littleworldwanderers.com/units/p/little-wanderers-preschool-2-week-free-trial

65.   Conduct Extensive Child Health Screenings
We will perform highly, qualified child health screenings, on a regular schedule, to
exceed the requirements to stay in compliance with the state's preschool licensing
laws. This will help to promote a culture of wellness within the facility. We will
develop a checklist to conduct and document these step-by-step procedures for
health screenings, and then communicate abnormal or unusual observations to
families and/or local health authorities.
Resource: https://mybrightwheel.com/blog/health-screening-for-preschoolers

66. **Value Diversity and Promote Inclusivity.**
We created a learning environment that is welcoming to children from many different backgrounds, and have incorporated diversity and inclusivity into the preschool's teacher training programs, educational philosophy and curriculum. Our objective will be to embrace and celebrate cultural differences, and train teachers to prepare children for a globalized world and foster empathy, respect, and inclusion.
Resource: www.himama.com/blog/teaching-diversity-in-preschool/
Example: https://thenestschool.com/blog/embracing-diversity-the-crucial-role-of-cultural-diversity-in-early-childhood-education/

67. **Promote Play-based Learning**
Emphasize the importance of play in children's learning and development, which allows children to explore, experiment, and learn at their own pace. The play-based learning is a hands-on, discovery approach, that also promotes the development of social and emotional skills. It allows children to use their imagination and creativity. Examples of play-based learning include playing dress ups, constructing building with blocks, singing songs, telling stories, playing with storage containers, cooking in a pretend kitchen, or having fun outside with sports games, or sand and water.
Source: https://mybrightwheel.com/blog/what-is-play-based-learning
Resource: www.education.wa.edu.au/play-based-learning

68. **Offer Specialized Programs Based on Child Talents**
We will offer programs that cater to children's unique interests and learning proclivities, such as language immersion programs, dual language, fitness, music and art classes, and STEM-focused curriculums. We will explore science, technology, engineering and math (STEM) concepts through picture books, games and related other hands-on-activities.
Resource: www.prosolutionstraining.com/resources/articles/8-ideas-for-incorporating-stem-learning-in-the-preschool-classroom.cfm
Source: www.stempreschoollearning.com/3-5-s-curriculum

69. **In-house Curriculum Coordinators**
Our in-house curriculum coordinators will specifically design our age appropriate, interactive lesson plans, that meet the needs of our children, with a focus on educational and social developmental activities.
Example: https://foundationspreschool.com/about-us/curriculum/

70. **Developed App to Assist with Child Behavioral Issues**
Our exclusive app offers strategies that guide children to positive behavior, in the classroom and at home. The app offers hundreds of age-appropriate strategies for teachers and parents to help children develop social, emotional, cognitive, and language skills, and behave in positive ways.
Example: www.pathwayslearningacademy.com/education/positive-behavior-support/

71. **Offer Special Education Services for Children with Disabilities**
We will provide programs that cater to individual child developmental and learning needs, and provide physical therapy, remedial speech, language instruction and mental health counseling.
Example: www.scoe.org/pub/htdocs/specialed-preschool.html
Directory Example:
www.privateschoolreview.com/new-york/special-education-private-schools/pre

72. **Strong Relationships with Local Businesses and Non-profit Organizations**
We will develop strong partnerships with other businesses and organizations in the community. We collaborate with local businesses, non-profits, and educational institutions to create a network of support and resources, that can benefit both the preschool and the wider community. We will work with businesses that understand how reliable and affordable high-quality childcare and preschool reduces the costs of employee absenteeism and enables parents to work or go back to school, either of which increases long-run employment and earnings potential. Our objective will be to get the business community and non-profit organizations to provide space and/or to share some of the operating costs of high-quality, early child development.
Source:
www.upjohn.org/research-highlights/why-businesses-should-care-about-childcare

73. **Perform Enhanced Background Checks on All New Hires**
We will take measures to hire staff who provide a safe, educational and nurturing environment for the children, while mitigating risk. We will work with background check companies that provide quality, fast and extensive checks. We will require Level 3 background checks, which will include criminal records, schooling, past employment, and reference checks.
Resources:
Checkr   https://checkr.com/
Use fine-grain filters to apply custom criteria, automatically and consistently, reducing adverse action rates.
Hire Safe   www.hiresafe.com/screening-solutions/background-check-solutions-
            by-industry/child-care-background-check/

74. **Multiple Facility Security Measures**
We will take the following security measures to improve the safety of the students:
a.   Motion-detected video surveillance in entranceways and community areas.
b.   Classroom video recording as a live feed to parents and build database.
c.   Front door controls (code, fingerprint scanner, interior door control)
d.   Front desk greeter and screener, with required visitors sign-in/out book.
e.   Entrance call box station outside front door
f.   Intruder breach alarms on all windows and doors
g.   Multiple panic buttons used by front desk and Director.
h.   Detailed evacuation and emergency handling plans
i.   Certified fire extinguishers throughout the facility
j.   Smoke and cardon dioxide detectors in every classroom and hallway.

k.   Regularly practiced fire drills.

l.   COVID protocols for cleaning and sanitation procedures.

m.   Baby monitoring in cribs.

n.   Verified child pickup only by authorized persons.

o.   Smart thermostats automatically control temperatures and enable remote access.

p.   Smart lighting system turns on lights when security system is disarmed.

Source: www.procaresoftware.com/blog/8-daycare-security-measures-you-need-to-take/
Example: www.green-roots.com/why-choose-us/security/
Resource: https://protechsecurity.com/keep-the-kids-safe-with-these-daycare-security-measures/

75.   Assemble an e-Portfolio for Every Student

We will create a domain for every student as a family communication tool. They can also take their e-portfolio with them, when they graduate, to carry a digital footprint that details their learner profile, learning assessments, drawing and writing samples, project notes, interests, teacher notations, references, memorable moments, milestone achievements, photos and written observations, awards, and other success stories.
Resources:
www.watermarkinsights.com/resources/blog/e-portfolio-tips-tricks-for-students
www.theempowerededucatoronline.com/2017/03/digital-child-portfolios.html/
Source:
https://mybrightwheel.com/blog/3-tips-to-make-curating-child-care-portfolios-easier
https://publuu.com/knowledge-base/student-portfolio/

76.   Mobile Party Services

We plan to be the local mobile rental resource for soft play, bounce houses, ball pits, party decorations, outdoor games, kids' tables and chairs, and painting and cooking stations. We will also become talent brokers and arrange for entertainment performances by clowns, makeup artists, DJs, photographers, jugglers, comedians, balloon artists, and magicians.
Example: https://www.happyhappysoftplay.com/
Photo Gallery   https://www.instagram.com/happyhappysoftplay/

Compare Competitive Advantages to Competitors

We will compare our competitive advantages to those of our primary competitors, and indicate if we are Better or (Worse), in each category. We will obtain and act upon the information about our competitors, from the following sources:

1.   Competitor Company Websites
2.   Review Sites, such as Google. Niche, Great Schools, Winnie, and Yelp
3.   Prior customers of our competitors
3.   Mutual suppliers
4.   Mystery undercover shoppers
5.   Posted internet articles by independent third parties.
6.   Social media account postings
7.   Business Directory and LinkedIn Listings

After completing this analysis, we will make certain to highlight what we do best, during parent tours, and in all our marketing materials.

XXXIII.   Preschool Marketing Strategies

Build an Informative and Interactive Website

Examples:

About Us

	https://naturalchoiceacademy.com/about/
Owner Welcome Letter	https://www.moed.bm/WKP/4629-Untitled.html
Backstory Video Message	
Education Philosophy	www.thefirstschool.org/about/preschoolphilosophy/
Curriculum	www.thefirstschool.org/ourprogram/
Partnerships	
Contact Us	www.premierlearningacademy.net/contact-us
Book a Tour	http://www.thefirstschool.org/admissions/
	https://app.acuityscheduling.com/schedule.php?owner=21853947&appointmentType=category:Tours
Enrollment Application	https://kidworksusa.com/enroll-your-child/
Distinguished Alumni	
Our Staff	www.thefirstschool.org/about/preschoolstaff/
Our Team	www.premierlearningacademy.net/faculty-staff
About Our Teachers	www.goddardschool.com/teachers-and-philosophy
Hours of Operation	www.premierlearningacademy.net/hours-of-operation
Photo Gallery	https://www.premierlearningacademy.net/gallery
School Year Calendar	www.littleexplorersdiscoveryschool.com/calendar
	https://kidworksusa.com/parents-corner/calendars/
Important Dates	www.premierlearningacademy.net/important-dates
Events	https://www.preschool-partners.org/events-1
Scholarship Program	www.littleexplorersdiscoveryschool.com/scholarship-program
Annual Report	https://grandviewkids.ca/about-us/annual-report/
	https://www.preschool-partners.org/annual-reports

Program Descriptions

Stay and Play	www.thefirstschool.org/ourprogram/stayplay/
Infant	www.cadence-education.com/programs/infant-care/
Toddler (12 to 36 Months)	www.cadence-education.com/programs/toddler-care/
Pre-K	
Preschool	https://mbskids.com/program/preschool-programs-in-houston/
After School Programs	https://kidworksusa.com/our-programs/after-school-care/
	www.littleexplorersdiscoveryschool.com/discovery-days-after-school-program
Summer Camp	www.littleexplorersdiscoveryschool.com/summer-camps

Enrollment
      How to Enroll
      Enrollment Process
      Registration
      Tuition
      Financial Aid   http://www.thefirstschool.org/financial-aid/
      Fundraising Events   www.thefirstschool.org/financial-aid/fundraising-event/

Parent Handbook
      Parent Resources   https://mbskids.com/preschool-activities/
      Rules and Regulations
      Parent Handbook   https://www.preschool-partners.org/parent-handbook
      Policies
      Awards   www.teacherspayteachers.com/browse?search=
             preschool%20awards%20certificates

      Safety Measures
      Security Systems
      School Holidays
      Competitive Advantages
      Technologies
      Pricing
      Referral Program   https://grandviewkids.ca/refer/
      Community Outreach   https://mbskids.com/community-outreach/
             www.thefirstschool.org/ourcommunity/communityoutreach/

Other Products/Services/Programs
      Rent Our Space
      Weekly Menu   https://kidworksusa.com/parents-corner/weekly-menu/
      Educational Toys/Games
      Children's Books
      Digital Downloads

Frequently Asked Questions   https://www.cadence-education.com/faqs/
Newsletter Archives   https://kidworksusa.com/parents-corner/stem-newsletters/
Newsletter Subscribe/Signup   https://www.naeyc.org/newsletter-signup
Parent Reviews   https://kidworksusa.com/parent-reviews/
Prominent Friends   https://kidworksusa.com/friends-of-kidworks-usa/
Video Tour of the Facility   https://www.youtube.com/watch?v=HrHTD6JAg2Q
Parent Testimonials   https://www.summitkids.com/testimonials-and-videos/
Teacher Video Testimonials   https://www.youtube.com/watch?v=x7IwDSasUug
Blog   www.littleexplorersdiscoveryschool.com/blog
      https://www.goddardschool.com/blog
Resources   www.littleexplorersdiscoveryschool.com/resources
Social Media Account Links   www.facebook.com/NaturalChoiceAcademy
      https://www.facebook.com/kidsrkidscorporate

	https://www.instagram.com/kidsrkidscorporate/
Referral Program	https://brightsideacademy.com/about-us/referral/
Family Feedback	https://www.goddardschool.com/family-feedback
Parent Satisfaction Survey	https://www.gfumc.com/preschool-parent-survey
Student Progress Report	www.lovetoknow.com/parenting/kids/printable-preschool-progress-reports
Employment	https://naturalchoiceacademy.com/employment/
Job Board	https://www.preschool-partners.org/job-board
Career Opportunities	www.littleexplorersdiscoveryschool.com/career-opportunities
Donate	https://alacarteeducationfoundation.org/
Volunteer	https://www.preschool-partners.org/volunteer
Franchise	https://wildrootsfranchise.com/
	https://www.goddardschoolfranchise.com/

Resources: www.squarespace.com   www.wix.com
              www.godaddy.com   www.shopify.com

Know the Best SEO Keywords

1. #Preschool   2. #Daycare
3. #Childcare   4. #Child
5. #Enrichmentprogram   6. #Kid
7. #Preschoolprogram   8. #Infantdaycare
9. #Childcarenearme

Market the Aspirational Dream

As an example, we will add a list of famous Montessori graduates, to our marketing materials, and make a note of their contributions to society:

Stephen Curry	NBA Four Time Champion Basketball Player
Julia Child	Chef, Author and TV Personality
Taylor Swift	Grammy Award Singer
Helen Hunt	Emmy Award winning actor
Gabriel García Marquez	Author, Nobel Prize in Literature recipient
Jeff Bezos	Amazon Founder
Sergey Brin	Google Founder
Larry Page	Google Founder

Source: https://amshq.org/About-Montessori/Montessori-Alumni
            https://themontessorifamily.com/the-most-famous-montessori-alumni/
            https://reachformontessori.com/famous-montessori-graduates/

Launch Free Class Trial Program

We will offer a free _____ (two day) trial of our preschool classes to realize the following business benefits:

1.   The set-up process may provide a lock-in opportunity, because parents will need to invest their time and energy to complete a modified registration application.

2. The parent will be asked to submit a completed survey at the end of the period, which will provide helpful feedback about the program and preschool.
3. For parents to assign value to this program, we will ask parents to cover the meal costs during the trial classes.
4. At the end of each session, conduct one-on-one interviews with parents, to collect data and answer questions.

Parents will benefit from the limited trial classes in the following ways:
1. Provides a risk-free way for parents to have their concerns and objections addressed.
2. Parents will receive the results of a basic child skills assessment, which will determine class positioning and curriculum fit.

We will use the following marketing tactics to promote this program:
1. Advertise that no credit card will be required.
2. Giveaway logo-imprinted T-shirts or school event highlighted calendars to encourage program sign-ups and promote the preschool.
3. Offer to give a minor, limited-time, tuition discount to parents who register their children on the last day of the free trial classes.
4. The company website will enable sign-ups for the free trial classes and post parent testimonials.
5. Upon parent release form submission, student in-class videos will be posted to social media sites.
6. A sidewalk sign and flyers will be used to promote this program.

Create a Google My Business Account
We will open this account to appear in Google searches and on Google Maps.
Resource: https://support.google.com/business/answer/2911778?hl=en&co= GENIE.Platform%3DDesktop

We will supply the following vital information to open this account: location, hours of operation, business name, description, contact name, phone number, website URL, business categories, etc.
Resource: www.podium.com/article/google-my-business-optimization/

To make our preschool stand out in Google searches, we will:
1. Make our listing very detailed by filling out all the available criteria.
2. Add high-resolution photos and videos to the listing.
3. Add a link to our website.
4. Continually educate and ask families on how-to post reviews about our preschool on Google.
      Resources: www.getweave.com/google-reviews/

www.podium.com/article/how-to-leave-google-review/

5.   Reply to all reviews to show that we value the feedback.
6.   Add posts, such as upcoming events, current industry news and blog updates about our milestone accomplishments, teaching philosophy and curriculum changes.
7.   Optimize local SEO by incorporating relevant keywords and location-specific terms. Such as preschool near me and after school enrichment programs.
8.   Enable Google Messages to allow families to communicate with our business.

Engage in Target Marketing

We will conduct cross-promotions with reciprocal referral partners, and circulate partner-only discounts or free one-day trial coupons to the following types of businesses, because they also service our ideal types of customers:

Realtors	Moving Companies
Chamber of Commerce Members	Pediatricians
Pediatric Dentists	Health and Fitness Clubs
Toy Stores	Children's Salons
Property Management Associations	Recreational Centers
Party Supply Stores	Gymnastic Centers
Karate Schools	Dance Studios
Studio Photographers	Children's Barber Shops
Private Elementary Schools	Daycare Centers
Community Centers	Preschool Associations
Child-related Non-profits	Nursery Furniture Stores
Telecommuters	Hybrid Companies
Kids Clothing Boutiques	Party Rental Equipment
Lego Stores	

Target New Moms

We will need to share the findings by the U.S. Department of Education, which states that children in high-quality preschool programs are more likely to develop high literacy skills. This prevents children from falling behind academically, ensuring that they keep up with their peers, and are more likely to graduate from high school and go on to college.
Fact: About 90% of new moms are millennials.

Target Marketing Strategies

1.   Join the Meetup and Facebooks Groups organized by new moms.
        Example: https://www.meetup.com/topics/new-moms/
2.   Provide personalized new mom postpartum coaching to help the transition to their new baby-centered lifestyle.
        Resource: www.newmom.me/blog/postpartum-coaches-why-all-new-moms-should-have-one
3.   Become a certified parent coach to provide a type of therapy where parents and caregivers learn how to use specific skills and strategies to address behavioral challenges and/or support their child's development.
        Resource: www.chconline.org/resourcelibrary/what-is-parent-coaching-do-i-need-it/

4. Write helpful, informative, relatable, uplifting content about caring for a newborn and oneself.
5. Become a Gender Reveal and/or Baby Shower Party Planner.
   Example: https://www.dreamarkevents.com/baby-shower
6. Become a sales consultant for In-Home Party Sales Companies that sell items for new moms.
   Example; www.mymommybiz.com/party/
   Directory: www.mommyhomemanager.com/10-great-direct-sales-companies-moms/
7. Work with known Millennial Influencers who target and connect with new moms and share their new mom related expertise and recommendations.
   Directory: www.clickanalytic.com/11-mom-influencers-to-follow-on-instagram-in-2024/
8. Become a mom blogger and develop affiliate marketing relationships with companies that sell new mom products, such as Amazon (https://affiliate-program.amazon.com/).
   Resources: https://twinsmommy.com/first-affiliate-sale-mom-blogger/
   https://www.authorityhacker.com/mom-affiliate-programs/
Resource: https://ahamediagroup.com/blog/5-ways-healthcare-marketers-can-engage-millennial-moms/

Install Front Yard Signage
We will supply students with the following types of front yard signage to celebrate student special occasions and accomplishments, while simultaneously providing greater exposure or visibility, in the neighborhood, for the preschool, with our imprint:
1. Student of the Month
2. Happy Birthday
3. Graduation Congrats
Resource: www.alphabetu.com/custom-products/signage-and-stickers/custom-yard-sign-congratulations-preschool-graduate

Publish a Parent Newsletter
We will publish printed and email versions of a Parent Newsletter to build long-term relationships with our customers and prospects. The newsletter will feature articles on the following topics:
1. Curriculum Updates
2. Teacher and Student of the Month
3. Director's Parenting Tip of the Month
4. Expert Child Health and Wellness Tips
4. Coming Events Calendar
5. Referral Program Winners
6. Games and Puzzles
7. Parents Questions and Answers
8. Noteworthy Accomplishments
8. Newly Posted Testimonials and Reviews

Self-Publish a Book
We will self-publish a book, that will be printed on-demand by Amazon Kindle

Direct Publishing, to demonstrate our early child development expertise, and improve our visibility with the targeted audience. We will give copies of this book to the parents who sign-up for our preschool tours, and to local reporters in our community.

Resource: https://kdp.amazon.com/en_US/bookshelf
Source: https://www.naeyc.org/resources/pubs/books/writing
               https://kindlepreneur.com/how-to-publish-childrens-book/
Example:
"Practical Wisdom for Parents: Raising Self-Confident Children in the Preschool Years." by Ellen Birnbaum (School Director (2008)- https://www.92ny.org/nursery-school) www.amazon.com/Practical-Wisdom-Parents-Self-Confident-Preschool/

Write a Newspaper Column
We plan to make an arrangement with the local newspaper, whereby our preschool would provide a regular column on practical advice to parents on child-rearing or children's developmental activities during the preschool years.
Resource: www.childcarenetwork.org

Launch a Partial Scholarship Program
We will establish and manage an annual budget line item for a partial scholarship program. This program will be funded from internally generated profits, and not use charitable contributions, which would require registering with state and federal authorities, and the filing of massive amounts of supporting legal documents. We will develop a 'tuition assistance cover letter', presenting information about our review and selection processes, and a 'partial scholarship application'. Financial need will be a prerequisite for receiving a partial scholarship, but other preferences will include: racial or cultural groups under-represented in the preschool, children with disabilities, and the siblings of returning or former students.

We will launch a partial scholarship program for the following reasons:
1. To give us reasons to issue press releases about the awarding of partial scholarships and build goodwill in the community.
2. To use the application process and information collected, to determine if the applicant qualifies for existing state or federal child care assistance programs or grants, which we will then use to help the parents to pursue.
3. To offer scholarships with varying degrees of benefits, from the waiving of the registration fee to having a portion of the weekly copay forgiven.
4. To gain a reputation for working with parents to make access to superior child care a reality for more families.
5. To realize the corporate tax benefits of such a program.
6. To widely promote in our marketing materials, the partial scholarship program as a competitive advantage.
7. To use the allocated funds in this account to offset bad debts or uncollectible tuition payments, as a means to maintain our community first image.

Examples: https://www.stjeromeecc.org/scholarship-information.html
               https://www.littleexplorersdiscoveryschool.com/scholarship-program

Source: www.theclassroom.com/military-child-scholarships-or-grants-13603673.html

Establish Relationships with Hospital Maternity Wards

We will research the hospital's website to determine their policies regarding new mom gifts, and whom to contact for approvals and alliance partnerships. Our objective will not be to make sales, or exploit the vulnerability of a new mom, but rather to gain recognition as a helpful, early child development resource.

We will then take the following actions:

1. Form alliances with services providers who have established access to maternity wards, such as baby photographers, and provide referral incentives for them to handout our brochures, and discount coupons.
    Resource:
    Accredited Professional Newborn Photographers International   https://apnpi.com/
    National Association of Portrait and Child Photographers   www.napcp.com/
2. Form cross-promotion alliances with sample product suppliers, such as educational toy and infant formula manufacturers.
3. Give marketing collateral to patient coordinators, nurses, new parents and their friends in the hospital waiting room.
4. Get hospital permission to distribute Baby Arrival Gift Baskets to new moms, with our included self-published book about parenting, toddler reading books and preschool enrollment discount coupons.
    Example: www.storkbabygiftbaskets.com/
5. Incorporate our preschool logo and marketing materials, into the gift basket packaging design, including red wagons, gift tin boxes, hampers, and woven baskets.
    Example: www.1800baskets.com/new-baby-gift-baskets-11085
6. Team up with other business that have valuable products for new parents and create an expanded baby pack with high value offers.
7. Form alliances with visiting Pediatricians and Postpartum Care service providers.
    Example: https://kidshealthfirst.com/public_pediatric_alliance/
    Source: https://theweek.com/articles/487400/disneys-disturbing-maternityward-marketing-scheme
    Resource: American Academy of Pediatrics   https://www.aap.org/

Align with New Mom Gift Basket Providers

We will contact local providers of gift baskets for new moms, and offer to provide them with our preschool logo-imprinted gift items or premiums, such as enrollment discount coupons, T-shirts, jewelry, blankets, school mini-backpack, baby books, gift certificates, skincare products, picture frames, slippers, fragrant candles, postnatal supplements, wipes, and educational toy subscriptions.

Examples:
https://www.amazon.com/new-mom-gift-basket/s?k=new+mom+gift+basket
https://www.newtonbaby.com/blogs/hush/postpartum-gift-basket
https://www.nurtured9.com/pregnancy-gift-box/p/hospital-bag-pregnancy-gift-box

www.cosmopolitan.com/style-beauty/fashion/g37405085/best-gift-baskets-for-new-moms/

Become a New Mom Coach

We will become a new mom coach to establish a trust-based, long-term relationship, with the new parent from an early point in time. The objective will be to form nurturing relationships, make valuable connections and share referrals. We will become experts in the following areas of concern by new moms: baby handling, bonding, soothing, diapering, bathing, skincare, nighttime sleeping, napping, breastfeeding, formula preparation, burping, swaddling and postpartum educating.

1. Write helpful articles for new moms:
   a. Diets for Breastfeeding New Moms
   b. New Mom Hacks
   c. Productivity for New Moms
   d. Personal Time Management for New Moms
2. Assemble Postpartum Gift Boxes

Resources: https://www.whattoexpect.com/first-year/newborn/
https://kidshealth.org/en/parents/guide-parents.html

Encourage More Reviews and Testimonials

We will regularly ask people who are known to be big fans of our preschool to submit testimonials and reviews about learning and progress, and to help build our trusted positive social proof fortress.
Resource: www.twinkl.com/resource/t-pa-663-parent-and-child-review-of-learning-template

We will use the following tactics to get more parent reviews:
1. Sign up with review websites, such as Google My Business, Facebook, and Yelp, and provide a link to the review form on our website and social media pages.
2. Encourage more reviews via our parent email newsletter and business email signature.
3. Talk to parents about how important it is for the preschool for them to submit reviews that convey how happy they are with their child's progress.
4. Conduct a prize drawing for parents who choose to leave their honest feedback on a participating review website.
5. Show parents that we value their feedback by promptly and positively responding to both negative and positive reviews, and make the warranted improvement changes, in a timely manner.
Resource: https://honestbuck.com/how-to-get-parent-reviews-for-your-daycare-business/

We will post our written reviews and video testimonials in the following places:

1.	Company Website	2.	Facebook Business Pages
3.	Instagram	4.	YouTube Channel
5.	Yelp	6.	Google Reviews
7.	Printed Marketing Materials	8.	GreatSchools.org
9.	Commonsensemedia.org		

Regularly Post to Social Media Accounts

We will make the following types of social media postings to establish our trustworthiness and resourcefulness:

- Ask parents to comment on past and suggested future preschool activities.
- Promote a future event, such as an open house or workshop.
- Provide photos of the student arts and crafts projects.
- Reshare or write a helpful parenting article about toddler raising tips.
- Update parents on the coming month curriculum theme.

Seize More Networking Opportunities

We will realize the following benefits from joining early childhood education associations:

1. Learn about industry trends and developments.
2. Qualify for recognized certifications and accreditations
3. Share information about best practices in early education.
4. Obtain grants, awards and scholarships
5. Attend educator training programs
6. Realize group buying discounts.
7. Secure more respected endorsements and reviews.
8. Share in a bigger pool of allocated resources.

List of Early Childhood Education Associations

National Association for the Education of Young Children	https://www.naeyc.org/
National Association for Family Child Care	https://nafcc.org/About-Us/
Council for Exceptional Children	https://exceptionalchildren.org/
National Head Start Association	https://nhsa.org/about-nhsa/
Association for Childhood Education International	https://ceinternational1892.org/
National Child Care Association	www.nationalchildcare.org/
Program for Infant Toddler Care	https://www.pitc.org/
National Resource Center for Health and Safety In Child Care and Early Education	https://nrckids.org/
Zero to Three	https://www.zerotothree.org/
Office of Child Care	https://www.acf.hhs.gov/occ

Directory: Center for Early Learning Professionals
https://center-elp.org/resourcesforms/national-early-childhood-organizations/

Produce More Targeted Marketing Videos

We will produce preschool marketing videos that accomplish the following goals:

1. To welcome parents to our preschool for a tour and consultation.
2. To give parents the opportunity to take a convenient virtual tour of the preschool, from the comfort of their own environment.
3. To capture parent testimonials that address a specific benefit, touch on a pain point, describes child benefits, and/or drives the viewer to take a prescribed action.
4. To give teachers and children a voice to express their joy with being associated with the preschool.
4. To produce a video blog (Vlog) to help the preschool to stand out as a parenting

or educating expert.
5. To use short-form or quick videos, on social media platforms, such as TikTok, Instagram Reels, YouTube Shorts, and Snapchat, to focus on being attention-grabbing or 'Edu-Taining' (educational and entertaining).
6. To convey the preschool's brand message, which embodies the essence of the school's philosophy, curriculum, core values, culture, or unique features and benefits that set it apart from the competition.
7. To show children at play, doing practical life activities, in the preschool classroom.
8. To feature videos of happy children enjoying their time at the preschool.
9. To show children performing a key lesson they learned, as a part of an end-of-semester recital.

Example: https://www.youtube.com/watch?v=Py4Xai2Jkks
Resources:
https://blog.lineleader.com/tips-for-using-videos-to-attract-new-childcare-leads
www.childcaresuccess.com/easy-child-care-businessvideo-marketing-ideas-thatwill-
    impress-parents/
https://bfsinc.net/using-video-market-childcare-company-preschool-montessori-school-
    private-elementary/

XXXIV.   Preschool Directory Sites

We will use the following directory listings to display contact options, location, competitive advantages, testimonials and/or our preschool photo gallery.

Resources:
Tootris   https://tootris.com/
It empowers working parents with powerful online resources to search, vet, and enroll their children in safe, nurturing, and affordable programs, all in real time.

Winnie   https://winnie.com/providers/
They have free and paid tools to boost enrollments and speed up admin tasks.

Trusted Care	https://trustedcare.com/
Angi	https://signup.angi.com/pro
Au Pair	https://www.aupair.com/en/preschools/country/usa.php
Buzz App	https://buzzapp.tech/
Care.com	https://www.care.com/business/
Great Schools	https://www.greatschools.org/
ChildcareAvenue.com	https://childcareavenue.com/provider/updateInfo.aspx
Child Care Central	www.childcarecentral.com/providers-register-login.php
Child Care Center	www.childcarecenter.us/provider
ChildCare.net	www.childcare.net/find-a-daycare/
DayCareResource.com	www.daycareresource.com/submit.html

MomTrusted.com	https://www.momtrusted.com/providers
Nextdoor.com	https://nextdoor.com/
Niche.com	https://www.niche.com/k12/search/private-preschools/
Paper Pinecone	https://www.paperpinecone.com/
Preschool Hub	https://preschoolhub.org/preschool-directory/
Private School Review	www.privateschoolreview.com/f
Yelp	https://www.yelp.com/nearme/preschool

Other Resources:
https://www.usnews.com/education/k12/preschool
https://childcare.gov/state-resources
https://en.wikipedia.org/wiki/Category:Preschools_in_the_United_States
Source: https://theearlychildhoodacademy.com/child-care-directories-need-listed/

XXXV.   Differentiation Strategies

Combine Co-working Space Rentals with Onsite Preschool/Daycare

We will offer to build onsite daycare and/or preschools in co-working space rental businesses to help support the work-life balance of professionals with families. We will also consider the reverse, and launch a co-working desk rental business in a vacant room in our childcare business. These types of arrangements will help to enhance member/parent convenience, engagement and retention, and generate additional revenue streams. We will tailor our childcare offerings to suit the unique needs of our members. We will of a unique blend of full-time daycare programs, part-time babysitting services, and educational enrichment activities to accommodate diverse family objectives and schedules. We will curate a supportive, childcare environment, that nurtures growth, creativity, and social development. We will soundproof or insulate the walls of the childcare area to control noise levels and design separate secure entranceways. We will create pricing options that will accommodate diverse member needs, including pay-as-you-go, monthly memberships, and incentives for regular users.

Source: www.spacebring.com/blog/member-experience/child-friendly-coworking
               https://www.optixapp.com/blog/childcare-and-coworking/
Examples: https://hackermoms.org/where-we-came-from/
               https://www.fandory.com/offices
               https://www.onespaceforall.ca/childcare
               https://www.childandcompany.com/

Focus on Meeting the Needs of the New Job Market Employers

Research indicates that the new job market will place a greater value on creative problem-solving skills and critical thinking. The goal will be to encourage more children to not be afraid to offer more innovative solutions, and become the future designers, writers, researchers, inventors and innovators. In fact, creative thinking skills are expected to be imperative for people who want to grow their businesses, progress in their careers, drive innovation, and experience a long-term sense of fulfilment and success, while not living with the fear of being displaced or made redundant by AI. We will develop a preschool curriculum that seeks to optimize the creativity potential of our students, while simultaneously developing their language and communication skills. We will develop experience-driven lessons that help to shape creativity and intelligence by promoting the student's growth mindset and a desire for continuous improvement. We will utilize technologies that enable more interactions between teachers and students, and teach students to view failures as positive learning opportunities.

Source: www.forbes.com/sites/rachelwells/2024/01/28/70-of-employers-say-creative-thinking-is-most-in-demand-skill-in-2024/

www.fastcompany.com/90818131/creativity-soft-skills-career-success-ai

The proposed curriculum will focus on the following types of activities to encourage the building of creativity-driven habits:

Painting	Cooking/Baking	Crafting
Fingerpainting	New Story Endings	Clay Modelling
Technology Integration	Dramatic Play	DIY Puzzle Making
Creative Role-Playing	Natural Materials Art	Collage Making
Paper Sculpting	Leaf Printing	Action Figure Play
Playing Dress-up	Expressive Dance	Building Blocks
Storytelling	Video Analysis	Creative Movement
Object Recycling	Playing Instruments	Drawing
Gardening	Singing	Puppets Play
Make Own Paint	Splatter Painting	

To better connect with early learners and develop a sense of curiosity, we will adapt the following strategies:

1. Encourage creativity by making available open-ended usage materials, such as play doh, building blocks and craft supplies.
2. Incorporate the child's favorite storybook characters into play scenarios.
3. Create a rotating schedule of 'play buddies' or 'group play' to appreciate the benefits of friendships, collaboration and teamwork.
4. Observe children at play to propose activities that align with their interests.
5. In group sessions, ask children to express their thoughts and feelings, on the subject matter, to foster a sense of self-worth and empowerment.
6. Develop lesson plans that are in sync with the attention spans and energy levels of the children.
7. Use songs, dance, games, puzzles, sports, and other movement activities to make learning a fun and engaging experience.
8. The playing of videos with the asking of questions about the content.
9. Give children the flexibility to express their creativity in different and multiple ways, such as via model storytelling, singing, dancing, building, painting, or sculpting.

Resources: www.kidkraft.com/us_en/blog/creative-art-activities-for-preschoolers

www.frogstreet.com/blogs/ideas-differentiated-instruction-in-early-childhood-education/

Source:
Examples:
www.theanimatedteacherblog.com/easy-differentiation-strategies/
https://bayareadiscoverymuseum.org/preschool/our-approach
https://raisingchildren.net.au/preschoolers/development/creative-development/preschooler-creative-activities
https://www.pinterest.com/happytotshelf/creative-learning-activities/

Turn Video Watching into a Learning Experience

We will teach students how to be actively involved with video presentations. We will train our teachers to incorporate video watching into lesson plans that feature interactive learning experiences. We will use the following techniques to foster visual learning and achieve these progressive goals:

1. State that the purpose for watching the video is to form a discussion group that allows a greater understanding of the story, information, and lessons presented in the video.
2. Occasionally pause the video, and build in deliberate reflective moments by asking questions that prompt students to evaluate whether they have been focusing on and understanding the material.
3. Occasionally stop the video to help the students to process and summarize the presented themes, ideas and activities.
4. Replay sections that help to provide answers to the questions being asked, such as:
   - What is the main story of the video?
   - Who is the hero of this video ….. and why?
   - Who is your favorite character ….. and why?
   - Which character do you not like …. and why?
   - What lessons have you learned from watching the video?
   - Where do you think this story takes place?
   - Who in this video is very happy … and why?
   - What happens at the end of the video?

Source:
www.edutopia.org/article/teaching-students-how-learn-videos/
www.educationworld.com/a_lesson/how-to-create-effective-lesson-using-video

XXXVI.   Expand the Monthly Family Statement

The expanded monthly statement will be auto-generated and emailed to families to stay better connected to the preschool. It will contain the following information categories:

1. Financial Account Statement
2. Student Progress Report
3. School News
4. Promotion Updates
5. Parent Feedback Template

Financial Account Statement

Opening Balance: Amount
Monthly Charges   Fixed Tuition Costs
                             Hourly Base Rate x Hours
                             Late Pickup Fees
                             Late Payment Fees
                             Afterschool Enrichment Program
                             Supply Purchases
                             Book/Toy Purchases
                             Specialty Lunches
                             Total:
Credits Earned   Discounts
                             Support Services Performed
                             Returns
                             Total:
Payments Made: Amount
Net Balance: Amount

Student Progress Report

School Days Attended
School Days Missed
Nap Time
Meal Time
Work Habits
Behavior Grade
Number Discipline Issues
Academics Scores
Observation Summary Code
Lesson Plan Code
New Skill Sets Learned
Major Achievement
Overall Student Evaluation
At-home Recommendations
Comments

School News

Teacher-of-the-Month
Student-of-the-Month
Referral Program Winner
Fundraising Program Results
Staff Changes
Enrollment Milestone Accomplished
Noteworthy Alumni Accomplishments

Promotion Updates

Afterschool Enrichment Programs

Summer Camp
Tutoring Programs
Pending Fundraisers
Enrollment Drives

Parent Feedback Template
Parent Satisfaction Surveys

Resources:
www.procaresupport.com/procare-desktop/docs/family-accounting-and-agency-reports
https://www.procaresoftware.com/blog/automate-childcare-billing-email-statements/
https://www.lillio.com/templates/daycare-daily-sheets
https://illumine.app/blog/daycare-reports-templates-and-tips/
https://childcaresoftware.webflow.io/templates
www.vancopayments.com/child-care/blog/daycare-tax-statements-receipt-templates
https://www.template.net/business/report-templates/preschool-progress-report/

XXXVII.   Track Preschool Key Performance Metrics

We will use the following financial and operational metrics (KPIs) to track the efficiency and financial health of our preschool business.

Average Daily Attendance =
Total Daily Attendance for Month / Total Number of Days Preschool Was Open
Example: 600 / 20 = 30 children per day

Children to Staff Ratio =
Total Number of Children / Total Number of Staff
Example: 30 / 5 = 6

Staff with Higher Education Credentials and/or Certifications
Number of Degreed or Certified Staff divided by Total Staff Number

Churn Rate
Number of Children Withdrawn / Average Number of Children
Example: 20 / 80 = 25%

Staff Retention Rate =
Number of Employees Retained / Number of Employees at Start of Period
Example: 36 / 40 = 90%

Children Retention Rate =

Number of children who stayed at the center over a certain period, divided by the total number at the beginning of that period, then multiplied by 100 for a percentage.

Full-Time Equivalency
Total Hours Attended by Children /Number of Available Full-time Hours
Example: 32 students x 10 P/T hours/week + 28 students x 30 F/T hrs week /
60 Potential Number of Chren x 30 F/T hours/week = 67%

Customer Acquisition Costs =
Sales and Marketing Costs / Number of New Enrolled Children
Example: $10,000 / 50 = $200.00

Profit Margin =
(Net Income divided by Total Revenue) x 100

Tour Conversion Rate =
Number of enrollment conversions divided by the total number of tour visitors.

Parent Satisfaction Scores
Feedback from parents provides valuable insights into the quality of care being provided. Also used to focus on score trends and highlighted problem areas that need to be improved.
Resource: https://info.ezchildtrack.com/blog/improving-customer-satisfaction-in-child-care-keeping-parents-happy

Total Cost per Child per Day =
Total Expenses for Year / Enrollment Number / Number of Days Open

Net Promoter Score
Percent of customers who are promoters – Percent who are detractors.
Purpose: Quantifies how well a business is managing its relationships with customers. Promoter scores = 9 or 10. Detractor scores = 6 or less.
Question: On a scale of 0 to 10, how likely are you to recommend us to a friend or colleague or family member?
Source: https://sharpsheets.io/blog/daycare-kpis-metrics/

XXXVIII.   Technologies Menu

Business Enhancing Technologies
We will purchase and maintain the latest technology to improve productivity, and efficiently enhance our office management, inventory management, payment processing, parent profiling, teaching platforms and record keeping systems.
Directory: https://www.capterra.com/child-care-software/

Preschool Management Software   www.ezcareonline.com
  Full enrollment & tuition management   Recurring billing
  Online parent payment portal   Student TimeClock
  Mass email communications   Executive Dashboard

Kangaroo Time   https://kangarootime.com/preschool-management
It helps users to optimize their center through automated billing, simplified classroom management, and streamlined parent engagement.

Smart Tuition   www.smarttuition.com

ProCare Software   www.procaresoftware.com
It provides real-time information for making critical decisions, maintaining compliance with local and state regulations, and adhering to business best practices.
Source: https://discover.procaresoftware.com/solutions-get-demo/

My Kid Reports
      https://mykidreports.mykidreports.com/preschools-management-software
Features automated billing, seamless online admission, efficient communication, and real-time child assessment.

Brightwheel Classroom Management App
      http://mybrightwheel.com/schools/#why-brightwheel
      https://mybrightwheel.com/childcare-management-software/
This childcare software automates administrative tasks, including billing and payments, enrollment management, communication with families, and tracking children's activities and development. It saves time, improves efficiency, and enhances communication between educators and parents.

My Kidz Day   https://www.mykidzday.com/
A childcare app for Parent Communication, Contactless Attendance, Temperature/Health Check and Enrollment Tracking for childcare, daycare, preschools, special needs, before and after care, and schools.

Marketing Software
ChildcareCRM   https://lineleader.com/
It automates enrollment and marketing, registers families online, communicates with families and staff, streamlines invoicing and payments, and offers comprehensive visibility into every contact throughout each stage of their enrollment journey.

Marketing 360   www.marketing360.com/marketing-software-for-child-care
It increases enrollment, books revenue, gets more reviews and retains clients from one platform.

Payment Processing
Rotessa   https://rotessa.com/resources/ach/ach-payments-for-daycares/

Google Teacher Productivity Enhancing Technologies

We will train our teachers to master the application of the following productivity enhancing technologies:

Google Drive	Used to store and share documents, images, videos and other files, from anywhere on the web (hosted in the cloud).
Google Docs	An online word processor used to create and format text documents.
Google Slides	An online presentation creating application.
Google Sheets	An online spreadsheet application that is used to track student homework and share the results with parents.
Google Forms	Used to create a form document or template, such as an assessment or survey, to publish to the web that will accept data and populate a spreadsheet.
Google Drawings	Used to create, edit and share drawings online.
Google Sites	Used to create and manage student e-portfolios, curriculum portals, and customized websites and webpages, without using HTML or other coding languages.
Google Calendar	Used to present the school's academic calendar, schedule school events, track project activities, share lesson plans, and send out invitations.
Google Classroom	Used to help teachers to efficiently create, organize, distribute and grade assignments, monitor student progress, and provide feedback to individual students.
Google Gmail	Used to send, receive and search emails, manage contact information, and create filters and labels.
Google Chat	Users can send, receive text, voice and video messages within the school district.
Google Talk	Enables guest lecture presentations and student video conferences, via video chat.
Google Groups	Used to form groups that encourage discussions among peer members, such as parent support groups.
Google Hangouts	Used to deliver lessons beyond the classroom walls, and save online interactions as an online portfolio building tool.
Google Translate	Helps users to overcome language barriers.
Google Blogger	https://support.google.com/blogger/answer/1623800?hl=en
Google Apps for Education	https://edu.google.com/intl/ALL_us/workspace-for-education/editions/education-fundamentals/
Google Teacher Academy	https://www.mcrel.org/google-teacher-academy/

Student Learning Technologies:

ABC Mouse   **www.ABCmouse.com**
It is a comprehensive digital learning resource for children ages 2–8. It is standards-based and includes thousands of learning activities, that are engaging and proven to be effective. It supports research-based best practices in early childhood education.

XXXIV.   Preschool Business Financing Options

We will explore the following types of business financing options:

1. Seller/Owner Financing
    Examples: www.bizbuysell.com/florida/broward-county/preschools-for-sale/
2. Leasebacks
    Resource: www.eeaspecialists.com/preschool-owners-is-sale-leaseback-the-key-to-financial-flexibility/
3. Investor Equity
    Resource: www.eeaspecialists.com/the-rise-of-preschool-private-equity-investments/
4. Venture Capitalist
    Example: https://sesameworkshop.org/our-work/research-and-insights/sesame-ventures/
5. Crowdfunding
    Example: https://time.com/3009460/crowdfunding-schools/
6. Home Equity Line of Credit
7. Credit Cards
    Source: www.nerdwallet.com/best/credit-cards/small-business
8. Personal Savings
    Resource: https://countingup.com/resources/advantages-and-disadvantages-of-personal-savings-in-business/
9. Family Borrowing
    Resource: www.comcapfactoring.com/blog/funding-sources-small-businesses/
                       www.usepigeon.io/
10. Bank or Credit Union Debt
    Example: https://www.nationalfunding.com/industries/loans/daycare-business/
11. Small Business Administration (SBA)
    Resources: www.sbaexpress.loans/blog/preschool-and-daycare-loans/
                        https://www.trademarcpreschoolrealty.com/financing
                        https://sba504.loans/sba-504-blog/sba-504-loans-for-preschools-and-daycare-centers/
                        www.sba7a.loans/sba-7a-loans-small-business-blog/using-the-sba-7a-for-a-preschool/
12. Roll Over Business Startup (ROBS)
    Resource: www.irs.gov/retirement-plans/rollovers-as-business-start-ups-compliance-project
13. Retirement Savings Account
    Resource: www.irs.gov/retirement-plans/plan-sponsor/types-of-retirement-plans
14. Alliances with Churches and Hospitals

	Example:	www.myfac.org/fellowshipministries/family-ministry/earlychildhood/
15.	Grants	
	Resource:	www.credibly.com/guides/daycare-loans-and-grants/
		www.playlsi.com/en/playground-planning-tools/resources/early-childhood-playground/funding/
16.	Fundraising	
	Resources:	www.vancopayments.com/child-care/blog/preschool-fundraising-ideas
		https://donorbox.org/nonprofit-blog/preschool-fundraising-ideas
17.	Franchising	
	Examples:	https://topfranchise.com/articles/the-top-12-preschool-franchise-businesses-in-usa/

Grant Prospecting Strategies

We will research the various ways to secure grant funding for our preschool.

Examples:

After-school Allstars   www.afterschoolallstars.org
A national non-profit organization that partners with schools across the nation to expand the learning day for low-income children.

Childcare Lounge   https://childcarelounge.com/pages/grants-for-early-childhood-education
Provides a directory of grant resources for preschools, including Lego's Children Grant Fund, Crayola Art Education Grants, and Kellogg Foundation.

Early Childhood Foundation   https://earlychildhoodfoundation.org/
An incubator of promising research and development projects that appear likely to improve the welfare of young children, from infancy through 7 years, in the United States. Welfare is broadly defined to include physical and mental health, safety, nutrition, education, play, familial support, acculturation, societal integration and childcare.

Instrumentl   https://www.instrumentl.com/browse-grants/grants-for-preschools
It helps preschools to get matched to relevant funders continuously. It provides grant management software and prioritizes opportunities with visuals, 990 summaries, and funder insights.

Preschool Franchising Models

Franchising will offer child care entrepreneurs a proven business model, operational support, and brand recognition. We will use this model to progress effectively and quickly in establishing first-class learning academies in communities with high interest and a need for our early childhood development services.

Kids R Kids International, Inc   https://kidsrkids.com/

This brand emphasizes a blend of education and childcare, with a focus on innovative curriculum and technology integration. Kids 'R' Kids has 85 employees, and the revenue per employee ratio is $114,286. Kids 'R' Kids peak revenue was $4.0M in 2023. The business was launched as a franchise in 1988, and they now have over 170 learning academies. It is based in Missouri City, Texas. They have a "Hug First, Then Teach" philosophy. They offer separate playgrounds for each developmental stage.

Source: www.zippia.com/kids-r-kids-careers-1252231/revenue/#
                https://www.franchisehelp.com/franchises/kids-r-kids/

Goddard Systems, Inc.   **www.goddardschool.com/**

Many consider Goddard the market leader in the children's daycare and preschool market and has been in the market since 1988. Their education philosophy is to provide current, academically endorsed methods to ensure that children have fun while learning the skills they need for long-term success. It is a franchisor with over 600 locations in 37 states, and is owned by Sycamore Partners, a private equity firm.

Resources: https://1851franchise.com/franchise-deep-dive-the-goddard-school-
                    franchise-costs-fees-profit-and-data-2721553#stories
                https://www.crunchbase.com/organization/the-goddard-school
                https://www.ibisworld.com/us/company/goddard-systems-inc/412901/

Children's Lighthouse Schools   **www.childrenslighthousefranchise.com/**

It has developed multiple revenue streams, including early childhood education, afterschool programs, summer camps and specialized programs. It has also created a proprietary STREAM-based curriculum.

Resource: https://1851franchise.com/childrens-lighthouse/the-top-5-reasons-to-buy-
                a-childrens-lighthouse-franchise-in-2024-2726323#stories

KLA Preschools
Montessori Kids Universe

Resource:
www.fmsfranchise.com/the-growing-preschool-and-educational-childcare-market-segment/

143

www.ingramcontent.com/pod-product-compliance
Lightning Source LLC
Chambersburg PA
CBHW071927210526
45479CB00002B/587

9798335114554